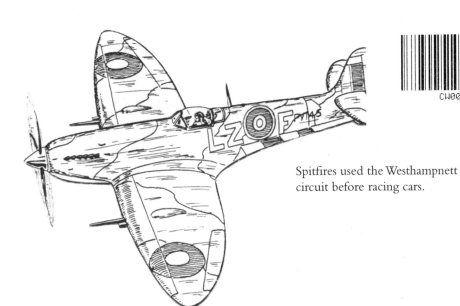

Spitfires used the Westhampnett circuit before racing cars.

Healeys were seen at the early meetings.

Aston Martins were very successful over the years.

1913 Bugatti, "Black Bess" at the circuit in 1955.

GOODWOOD

Remembered

1948–1960

GOODWOOD
Remembered

Peter Redman

All drawings, cartoons, sketches, and most photographs by the Author

Pages from the Goodwood programmes reproduced by kind permission of the BARC

Published by:

IM Publications, 6 Charlton Mill, Charlton, Chichester,
West Sussex PO18 0HY, UK. Tel: +44-1243-811334,
Fax: +44-1243-811711, E-mail: info@impub.co.uk,
Web: www.impublications.com
Book website: www.goodwoodremembered.com

Cover photograph © The Klemantaski Collection
"Goodwood" and "Festival of Speed" are trademarks of
The Goodwood Estate Company Limited

ISBN: 978-1-901019-06-3
British Library Cataloguing-in-Publication Data
A catalogue record for this book is available from the
British Library

Designed by SCW www.scw.uk.com
Printed in the UK by Biddles Limited

Contents

Driver profiles

Acknowledgements

My thanks to Keith Goffe for his friendship, help, proof reading, and his introductions to many very interesting and helpful people. Also, his endless stream of good ideas and his willingness to provide a quality taxi service for the many trips we did to Goodwood and elsewhere during the production of this book. Without all this, my book might never have reached publication. Also, to Alan R. Smith (motor racing photographer) for his friendship, vast knowledge, which he is always willing to share, and his encouragement during the early stages of this project.

To the many people who were kind enough to read the draft copy, give me their honest opinions and guide me in the right direction, particularly Sir Stirling Moss and Roy Salvadori. Also, authors Louis Connolly and Tony Gardiner, and motor racing photographer Peter Collins for their comments and suggestions at a crucial stage of production.

Particular thanks to historic motoring journalist, author, and historic racing car driver Ed McDonough for his comments and enthusiasm, and for writing a Foreword for this book. Likewise to Willie Green.

My thanks to Colin, Barry, Stephanie, and the rest of the staff at Petaprint for the mountains of photocopying over many months and to Gary, Kate, and the others at Petersfield Photographic for producing highly presentable copies from some of my old and rather tatty photographs in the early stages of this project.

Thanks to Chris Saville (AROC) for very useful information and to James McNaughton (Sec. GRRC) and his staff for their enthusiasm and to all those who had faith in me and who placed orders for it long before the book was completed.

My thanks to Lord March for granting permission for the use of the name "GOODWOOD" in the title. Also, to Jeannie Perkins and Lynn Cheesmur, at Goodwood, for their help and assistance.

My thanks to Alan R. Smith, Trevor Redman, and Peter Dyer for supplying additional photographs.

The pages in this book taken from early Goodwood Programmes are reproduced with kind permission of the British Automobile Racing Club (BARC).

The following publications were an essential part of my research for facts, figures, and other details. I was so glad to have them to hand on my bookshelves:

Mike Lawrence, Simon Taylor and Doug Nye, *The Glory of Goodwood*. Virgin Books, London (1999).

Peter Garnier, *Goodwood*. A National Motor Museum Trust book, Dalton Watson Ltd, London (1980).

Louis Klemantaski and Michael Frostick, *Motor Racing Circuits of Europe*. B.T. Batsford, London (1958).

David Weguelin, *The History of E.R.A.* New Cavendish Books, White Mouse Limited Edition (1980).

Giovanni Lurani, *A History of Motor Racing*. Hamlyn Publishing Group Ltd, London (1972).

Karl Ludvigsen, *Stirling Moss*. Patrick Stephens Ltd, Sparkford, UK.

Mike Lawrence, *Four Wheel Drift—1945–1959*. Greville Publishing Co. Ltd, London (1994).

Wayne Mineau (Ed.), *Stirling Moss's Book of Motor Sport*. Cassell and Co. Ltd, London (1994).

Alan R. Smith, *Fifties Motor Racing*. Haynes Publishing Group, Sparkford, UK (1990).

Stirling Moss and Doug Nye, *Stirling Moss*. Patrick Stephens Ltd/Thorsons Publishing Group, Wellingborough, UK (1987).

W. Boddy, *Brooklands*. Grenville Publishing Co. Ltd, London (1950).

Also my (incomplete) collection of period BARC Goodwood Programmes.

And finally, a very big "Thank you" to Ian Michael (the Publisher) who has put in a lot of effort and a great deal of his own, valuable time to bring all of my vintage and, in many cases, rather poor photographs up to the standard which you will see in this book. Without this, some would have been thought to be just not good enough and discarded. G

Dedication

To Frankie, my Wife, who has put up with me for more than 50 years.

I thank her particularly for her patience and understanding during the past couple of years or so and especially the last few months while work on this book began to take me over.

Also, to our children and grandchildren, who were the inspiration for the first few scribblings, which led ultimately to this becoming a book. G

Goodwood House in 1952 when Frankie and I had a conducted tour of the house and grounds when we were members of a group on a Southdown coach excursion from Bognor Regis.

GOODWOOD

PETER COLLINS
COOPER 500

REG PARNELL   B.R.M.

LAVANT
CORNER

LAVANT STRAIGHT

WOODCOTE
CORNER.

STIRLING MOSS   H.W.M.

ST. MARY'S

PADDOCK BEND.

START AND
FINISH

FORDWATER

MADGWICK CORNER

MIKE HAWTHORN   THIN WALL SPECIAL

GIUSEPPI FARINA   ALFA-ROMEO

A quick sketch from 1958.

Foreword by Ed McDonough

European Editor of *Vintage Racecar*
Motor Racing Historian, Journalist, and Author

As a motor racing historian, I spend a significant amount of time searching for first hand accounts of what happened at various times during the past hundred years. While a great deal of history of "our" sport has been recorded in writing and photographs, it has to be remembered that the larger share still remains in peoples' heads... and in their lofts!

One of the best things I ever hear is when someone says "I found this box of old racing photos my dad took at Goodwood"... or Silverstone or Le Mans or any number of other racing venues. As an author, I have always thought it a bit special to be able to use accounts or photos taken at some obscure race meeting in the '50s. There's something interesting about using the photo a fan took of a driver fifty years ago and kept for all that time. Sadly, those photos and people are beginning to be in short supply.

It's good fortune, then, that enthusiasts like Peter Redman are still around, and that they hung onto their own memorabilia, and collected more. And Peter has the added fortune to be able to convert his memories into drawings that somehow capture that bit more than photographs can.

The resurrection of the Goodwood circuit and the Festival of Speed in recent years have sparked a number of written accounts of racing at the Sussex circuit. There are some quality professional books on Goodwood now, but there still is nothing quite like hearing the experiences of the people who were there "on the day". The race reports will never capture what happened round the back of the circuit when Roy or Stirling spun and went to talk to the crowd at the fence, or what the mood of the spectators was about parking facilities of the day, or how thousands had to manage with one or two loos! The raw data of history is always important, but the "feel" and subjectivity of it is just as significant, perhaps more so.

Peter's photos, drawings, cartoons, and recollections bring back the reality of the post-war Goodwood days. This is a modest book in size and scope, but it has that "I was there" feeling. Motor racing history will be safe as long as we continue to have access to the reality of the "good old days". G

Foreword by Willie Green
Historic Racing Car Driver for more than 30 years

Fifty years ago when I was at Prep School, there were three or four of us who would listen to the radio reports of Le Mans and various Grand Prix. We are still in touch today, but it never occurred to me that one day I would not only drive the actual cars that we were listening to but also get to know most of the drivers that survived.

Regrettably there were so many fatalities in those days, the circuits were not the anaesthetised "Go Kart" tracks we are presented with nowadays; the spectators didn't need binoculars and on occasion even became part of the action.

Looking at the photographs in this book will transport you back to the days when motor racing was a "sport", a real hobby and heroes were available in the paddock. Racing cars were brought on the back of old trailers and teams would even help the opposition!

Goodwood remains the only circuit whose profile remains almost the same as the original layout. Though the chicane is now tighter, with the original high speed corners the Earl of March has more than recaptured the Spirit of Goodwood with the Revival meetings.

Enjoy it while you can; remember that it was closed in 1966 because it was too fast and I have personal experience that most of the "original" cars now have at least 25% more power. Happy memories. G

Introduction

As a small boy in the late 1930s, I remember overhearing a conversation between my parents, an uncle, and a family friend, recounting their experiences after a visit to Brooklands to watch the motor racing. Their descriptions of the day's events which they had witnessed, were so vivid that I vowed to go there as soon I was old enough. Unfortunately, the Second World War intervened.

Eavesdropping on grown-ups' conversations can have a profound influence on a small boy, and I started collecting books on motor racing and looked forward to the day when the war would end so that Brooklands could open its gates once more. Needless to say, I was mortified when I heard the news that this was not going to happen. But I was overjoyed in 1948 when it was known that a motor race meeting was planned to take place at nearby Goodwood (we lived in Bognor Regis at the time) and that it would be run on similar lines to those at Brooklands pre-war. I regret that I never experienced the thrill of the sights and sounds of the famous Surrey track in its heyday, but did the next best thing by becoming a member of the Brooklands Society soon after it was founded. I have attended many events there over the years as a member of the society and I have driven my 1924 Trojan and 1936 Daimler on its hallowed concrete.

However, I went to that first Goodwood meeting in 1948 and became a regular and very enthusiastic spectator. In the 1950s, we were young and hard-up and on occasions resorted to getting into the circuit by crawling through the hedge (apologies to Lord March). I had a very basic camera in those days and used it whenever we were at the front of the crowd. But I made good use of it on practice days when we were allowed into the paddock to mingle with the "stars" and their machines. I managed to get a few reasonable pictures from time to time and these were duly stuck into albums.

I was greatly thrilled when I drove my Trojan round the circuit in the parade of vehicles and took part in the driving tests during the 1963 International Veteran and Vintage Car Rally. Also, I was proud to be one of the many Goodwood Supporters during all the trials and tribulations in the years before permission was at last granted to Lord March to open the circuit once again for motor racing. The vivid memories of Goodwood in those early days will be with me for the rest of my life; of remarkable drivers racing fantastic machines on a small racing circuit in the most beautiful part of the English countryside. A combination, the like of which I believe not to be found anywhere else in the world.

I started on this project while recovering from a spell in hospital and was not allowed to attempt anything too physical. The thought of it becoming a book had not entered my head. It was to be nothing more than a few random jottings for the benefit of our grandchildren, to let them know how much fun my wife and I had had watching motor racing in a bygone age. When I was about halfway through (*I thought*) I asked my good friend, Alan, for his opinion as he knew Goodwood very well. On returning the rough draft to me, he made the comment that I should include some of my sketches and that it might then be worthy of publication.

This meant a search in the loft to find them. Upon inspection I realised that some were rather scruffy and that others had not been too good to start with. This would mean reworking most of them. However, I put off doing this while I carried on with text. To help with this I dug out my collection of old Goodwood programmes, some were a bit worse for wear and others had gone missing. But those which I did have were very useful and I was very pleased that I had kept them for all those years. More and more pages fell out of the printer as I found that writing about any one event triggered off the memory cells in all directions, and I could not work my fingers fast enough on the word processor. At last I decided that enough was enough and called a halt, put it on one side, and took a long hard look at the sketches.

Some were not too bad and needed only a little tidying up, so I set about this task next and found that it did not take that long. Those precious skills had not deserted me after all. I then set about redrawing most of the rest. While in the loft searching for the sketches, I had stumbled across a box containing the old photo albums and thought that it might be an idea to include some of the better pictures. Over the years, the albums had begun to fall apart and as they contained photographs of VCC London to Brighton runs and other Veteran and Vintage events, I decided that the time had come to dismember them and put all the Goodwood pages together.

I realised that many of the photos were not good enough for any thoughts of publication, so had them enhanced with the aid of modern technology and the skills of the people at Petersfield Photographic. As things progressed, another friend and real Goodwood

enthusiast, Keith, came up with many good suggestions and introduced me to several very interesting and helpful people. He had seen the small selection of photographs, which I had included so far but when I showed him the rest of the album pages he said, "They *must all* be included in the book" and so they are, warts and all.

I hope that you will enjoy reading this book and studying the pictures half as much as I have enjoyed writing it and putting it all together. G

The Pits, September 1954, Practice Day

The car nearest the camera is a 250F Maserati—one of three at that meeting.

The Thin Wall Special and the Vanwall Special at rest. Peter Collins resting on the tail of the Vanwall. On race day, Collins finished second in this car in the Goodwood Trophy and then won the Woodcote Cup driving the Thin Wall Special. Mike Hawthorn, driving the Vanwall Special finished fourth in the Woodcote Cup. It looks like Mike Hawthorn coming through the Paddock gate.

Chapter 1

Reg Parnell, Maserati 4CLT/48, in the process of winning the first ever Formula 1 race held at Goodwood, followed closely by second man home, Bob Gerard, in his 1938 ERA R14B.

Birth of a legend

18th September 1948 is a date engraved on my mind and one of the most exciting that a teenager could have experienced. It was the occasion of the first motor race meeting using the Westhampnett Airfield perimeter track, to be known as Goodwood. The history of this famous circuit has been recorded many times by far more knowledgeable souls than me, so I will not even attempt it. This is just an account of how I remember the many enjoyable hours I spent there over the first 12 years of the circuit's existence. Usually this was in wonderful "Goodwood" weather, but sometimes in the pouring rain. But even then the experience was enjoyable.

My first visit was by courtesy of my elder brother's friend, Brian Johnson. He owned a car (a 1936 Triumph Vitesse) and had invited my brother, also Brian, and our cousin, Rae, to accompany him to this historic function. Fortunately, he knew of my interest in motor racing and very kindly invited me along too. I was only 16 years old at the time, and was a little surprised but, of course, only too pleased to accept.

That first meeting was blessed with fine weather and, having parked the car with all the others in a field nearby, we made our way, with dozens of other excited spectators, to the eastern end of what we know now as the Lavant Straight. Brian Johnson had done some research and decided that this was the best place from which to see the action. From this position, behind nothing more than a piece of rope strung between iron stakes, we were able to see the cars approaching at speed and then braking hard as they swept into Woodcote corner. They would then accelerate down the start and finish straight, rear tyres smoking and cars snaking as drivers tried desperately to be first into Madgwick corner.

We watched the first two races from this position and then realised that some of the crowd had found an even better vantage point. They had climbed onto the roof of one of the old, war time RAF buildings. So we joined them. We had a marvellous view for the next race. We could see the whole of the Lavant Straight and even Fordwater across the airfield. We even enjoyed half the following race from here, but were then told by the officials, in no uncertain terms, to come down to earth.

With hindsight we were lucky that we all lived to tell the tale, as the roof, which was supporting about a dozen of us, was made of corrugated asbestos supported by quite flimsy pieces of old timber. Of course, by now our original places had been taken by others, so we walked towards Lavant Corner and found a good spot about halfway along the Lavant Straight behind some chestnut fencing (which was marginally safer). We spent the rest of that fantastic day there and enjoyed every moment.

The first race of the day, which was, of course, the first ever race on the Goodwood Circuit, was won by one Paul Pycroft driving his Pycroft Jaguar, which was a pre-war SS100 fitted with a streamlined body designed and built by the owner. This was a good omen for what was to come in the following years. Goodwood was following in the footsteps of Brooklands—Hooray!!!!

I had been interested in motor racing in general and Brooklands in particular since I was about five years old, but was too young to attend. Then Hitler put a spanner in the works.

The news, at the end of the war, that Brooklands was not going to re-open for motor racing had brought tears to my eyes. However, now Goodwood was taking over.

The field for that first meeting was full of ERAs, some Maseratis, an Alfa Romeo, a gaggle of HRGs, some MGs, and a Morgan (driven by Peter Morgan). Most of these dated from pre-war, but one race, which had spectators jumping up and down, was for a new, post-war breed; that for cars with engine size of just 500 cc. These diminutive racing cars with modified motor cycle engines mounted behind the driver were to play a big part in the story of Goodwood and other circuits around the country for several years to come. They were great fun to watch and being very evenly matched in performance, provided a more exciting spectacle than that sometimes produced by the more powerful cars.

Reg Parnell

The undisputed "King" of Goodwood in the early days, "Uncle Reggie" was a very popular driver as well as a very successful one. Between 1948 and 1956 he won a total of 15 races, eight of these with his trusty 4CLT Maserati. He had two wins and a second place with the V16 BRM, and with the famous Thin Wall Special he clocked up two more wins, two seconds, and a third place.

With co-driver Eric Thompson, Reg Parnell won the second Nine-hour race in 1953, driving an Aston Martin DB3S. During 1954 Parnell had two wins and two third places with his Ferrari 500. Over the years he drove a variety of other cars including Cooper and Connaught.

After a brilliant driving career he became equally successful as Team Manager for Aston Martin.

18th September 1948
Daily Graphic five-lap Formula 1 race for the Goodwood Trophy.
Reg Parnell (Maserati 4CLT/18), winner, at Madgwick.
Bob Gerard (ERA R14B), second.

Event 5, which was for just such machines, was a wonderful scrap between a handful of drivers of whom we would see a lot more in the future and was a curtain raiser on the Cooper marque at Goodwood. This race was won convincingly by a young man destined for greatness. In a three-lap race, he finished with a 25 second lead over second man, Eric Brandon, himself no slouch. The winner, Stirling Moss, was just 19 years of age.

Third place went to Curly Dryden, four seconds behind Brandon. All three were driving Cooper cars.

The list of drivers at this first meeting reads like a page from motor racing's "Who's who":

Reg Parnell (Maserati 4CLT/48)
Duncan Hamilton (Maserati 6CM)
Bob Gerard (ERA B-Type)
John Bolster (ERA B-Type)
Peter Walker (ERA B-Type)
David Hampshire (ERA A-Type)
Cuth Harrison (ERA C-Type)
Geoffrey Ansell (ERA B-Type)
Dennis Poore (Alfa Romeo 8C/35)
Dudley Folland (MG K3)
Frank Kennington (MG K3)
and, of course, many more.

At the end of the meeting, as spectators made their way back to the "car park", I remember to this day the buzz of excited talking and the fact that everyone had smiles on their faces. Complete strangers engaged in animated conversation. As we waited our turn in the chaos to leave the field, no one got angry with the driver in front or the one who tried to push in. All was taken in good spirit and we had a good laugh about the fact that it seemed that many more people had turned up than were expected. The four of us returned home tired but elated. Our parents and

friends had to put up with days of endless chatter as we recounted the events of that fantastic day, over and over again.

We were not alone in eagerly looking forward to the next "Goodwood" meeting. This took place on Easter Monday, 18th April 1949. I had to resort to pedal power and use my trusty Raleigh, as Brian Johnson was taking a young lady in his car! But it was only about six miles and I had been cycling those country lanes for the last five years and knew them well.

This, second, meeting had a very similar line up to the first, but with a few "new" faces and cars.

Dudley Folland had found himself a Ferrari 166 with which he won the first race of the day. Leslie Johnson finished third in Event 3 and fifth in Event 5 in an ERA. Tony Rolt was driving an Alfa Romeo and Fred Ashmore had a Maserati 4CLT/48 as a matching pair to that of Reg Parnell.

Stirling Moss won Event 6, a handicap race, driving his Cooper-JAP T9. In this event, George Abecassis finished third driving a

ERA R14B
A pre-war racing car driven successfully at Goodwood by Bob Gerard.

Cooper-Vincent T9, having previously finished sixth in Event 5 driving an Alta.

The September meeting of 1949 saw only two races for sports cars, whereas the previous year, four events were for "more or less" everyday machinery.

Goodwood was evolving and a pattern was beginning to develop. At this meeting the silverware was carried off by Stirling Moss, Reg Parnell, Peter Collins, Ken McAlpine, Tony Rolt, Gordon Shillito, and Gerry Dunham. Most of them would become regulars at doing just that.

The 500 cc and 1000 cc races always produced some thrills and sometimes some spills.

At the 1949 September meeting, Coopers filled the first three places in both these events. In the races for the heavy machinery, pre-war ERAs were still very much in evidence. However, it was the 500 cc class which produced some of the closest and therefore most exciting racing in the early years. In some races, most of the cars taking part were Coopers, though not all had the same power units. Most were fitted with JAP engines, but there were those with Norton, HRD, and others.

At the 1950 September meeting, Coopers were driven by John Cooper himself, Stirling Moss, Eric Brandon, Peter Collins, Reg Parnell, Alan Brown, Curly Dryden, and Alf

Photographers love to get near to the action

Bottoms. Don Parker drove his Parker-JAP Special and Paul Emery had two of his Emeryson cars entered. He drove one and Frank Kennington the other. These were unusual in this class in that their engines were in front of the driver.

J.M. Sparrowe built and raced his Sparrowe-Marwyn-Special and Spike Rhiando did likewise with his Rhiando-Trimax.

In 1951 two JBS 500s were entered by James Bottoms, one driven by Alf Bottoms and the other by Frank Aitkens. Les Leston entered and drove a third. Also, in 1951 Stirling Moss was seen driving a Kieft-Norton in this class and in 1952 we saw Bob Gerard and Ken Wharton both driving Cooper 500s. Quite a change from their usual high-powered mounts.

Among my rather poor photographs, is one of a young Ken Tyrell driving a Cooper 500 in 1956 (page 78).

The variety of makes in these classes added interest for the spectator and, in the right hands, a Kieft could be more than a match for the all-conquering Coopers. When Stirling Moss or Don Parker was driving a Kieft, then we knew that it was a race really worth watching. G

18th September 1948: three-lap race for 500 cc cars. Stirling Moss (Cooper-JAP), winner, at Fordwater. Eric Brandon (Cooper-JAP), second, Curly Dryden (Cooper-Norton), third.

The good in Goodwood

The Easter meetings at Goodwood were always most enjoyable, partly because of the time of year, but also because the programme was bound to contain some different cars and drivers from the previous year for the spectators to cast their eyes over.

The atmosphere in the enclosures was always friendly and cheerful and on occasions could be almost "party-like". Complete strangers would become good friends for the day and "hope to meet again sometime".

After the long English winter, spring and a new motor racing season were about to burst into life. The buzz of excited chatter, which started in the car parks as the enthusiastic crowd arrived and made its way to the turnstiles, swelled considerably as the enclosures and stands filled as the time for the first race drew near.

Easter 1954
Reg Parnell in the pit area with the Ferrari 500 with which he won the Lavant Cup, seven-lap Formula 1 race, on race day. Roy Salvadori was second in the Gilby Engineering 250F Maserati with Ken McAlpine third in a Connaught.

The Easter Monday meeting of 1950 (10th April) had plenty of interest for the spectator. In the races for the Chichester Cup and the Richmond Trophy, as well as those who were becoming "Goodwood regulars", the entry list included Prince Bira and Baron de Graffenried, both driving 4CLT Maseratis. Peter Whitehead had a Ferrari and, for the Chichester Cup only, Stirling Moss and George Abecassis were in HWM-Altas.

In the Chichester Cup, Bira lead from start to finish with the Baron close behind, and Dennis Poore third in his big Alfa Romeo, ahead of Reg Parnell in his 4CLT. However, Parnell got his own back in the Richmond Trophy race by winning from de Graffenried,

with Brian Shaw-Taylor coming third in his trusty pre-war ERA R9B.

Event 1 at this meeting was a five-lap scratch race for the Lavant Cup. This was for cars of up to 2000 cc non-supercharged and up to 1100 cc supercharged. There were a number of little Coopers with a variety of 1000 cc engines up against HWMs, two supercharged MGs, a Frazer Nash, HW Alta, Healey, and several others. The little Coopers came home first, second, and third. The drivers were: Bill Aston (JAP T9), Eric Brandon (JAP T12), and John Green (Vincent HRD T12).

Handicap races were always good fun to watch and gave drivers of the less powerful machinery and those with less experience a

Easter Monday 10th April 1950
It was rather damp for the 11-lap Richmond Trophy Formula 1 race. Baron de Graffenried, who finished second to Reg Parnell in a similar Maserati 4CLT, is pictured splashing his way round Woodcote followed by Brian Shaw-Taylor in his ERA R9B who finished third.

The Friary Mobile Bar
A regular and welcome sight at Goodwood and other events around the area at that time.

sporting chance. They provided great spectacle and sometimes produced unlikely race winners. The First Easter Handicap of 1950 finished: first Bill Aston (Cooper 1000), second B. de Lissa (1087 cc supercharged MG) and third Gerry Dunham in his famous Alvis Special with 1842 cc engine. Quite a variety!

The progress of some drivers through the field in these handicap events was quite phenomenal. Tony Rolt in the ERA-Delage in the First Whitsun Handicap in that year is a very good example. He had only a 15 second start over scratch man Brian Shaw-Taylor's ERA and started 95 seconds behind Haesendonck's MG, with nine cars between them. In a five-lap race on a small circuit, the way he carved his way through the field was fantastic to watch.

By the end of the first lap he had passed three cars and was in eleventh place. By the end of lap two he was eighth, lap three he was seventh and by the end of lap four, he was in third place, where he finished. To pass three cars on one lap at Goodwood is great but to

do it twice, in a five-lap race is unbelievable. I was there and saw it happen.

The Whitsun meeting that year centred around the 500 International Trophy. This was for racing cars of not more than 500 cc and was the biggest Formula 3 event as yet held in Europe. It took the form of two heats and a final. Rolling starts were a feature, with the race cars holding their grid positions behind a "Pilot" car for the "Pilot" lap and the race started when the "Pilot" car pulled off the track by the Paddock "in" gate and the flag was dropped.

Twenty cars with the best times from the two seven-lap heats then took part in a 15-lap final. Eric Brandon won the first heat in his Cooper-Norton, with Peter Collins in another Cooper-Norton in second place. Dennis Poore was third in a Parsenn-JAP. Heat 2 saw Curly Dryden win in another Cooper-Norton. Second place went to W.J. Whitehouse in yet another Cooper-Norton and Don Parker finished third in his Parker-JAP Special.

The final was fast and furious, as usual with 500 cc racing, with all the drivers at 100%.

The Ferrari 500 driven by Reg Parnell and entered by Scuderia Ambrosiana photographed at the September meeting 1954.

Peter Collins

He first raced at Goodwood in September 1949 and won the race for 500 cc cars driving a Cooper-Norton. Over the next nine years he went on to show that he was as versatile as anyone by finishing in the first three places with Cooper-JAP, Aston Martin, Thin Wall Special, Vanwall, BRM P30, and Ferrari. He won the 1952 Nine-hour race with co-driver Pat Griffiths in a DB3 Aston Martin, and the pair came second in the 1953 event driving a DB3S. With the Thin Wall Special, he won the 1954 Whitsun Trophy and the Woodcote Cup at the September meeting. On Easter Monday 1955 he carried on his winning ways by winning the Chichester Cup driving a P30 Mk II BRM. The third of the trio of great British drivers of the time with Stirling Moss and Mike Hawthorn, it was very sad that his life was cut short just as he reached his true potential and looked like a future World Champion.

17th September 1949, five-lap race for 500 cc cars
Peter Collins (Cooper-Norton), winner, at Woodcote.
Lex Beels (Cooper-JAP), second, Stan Coldham (Cooper-JAP), third.

My first attempts at photography at Goodwood, September 1950
The V16 BRM driven by Reg Parnell in the process of winning its first ever race, the five-lap Woodcote Cup in very wet conditions (left). Peter Whitehead making some "in race" adjustments to his ERA R10B (right).

There were a number of excursions onto the grass at various places around the circuit and several retirements. However, it was another good day for the Cooper marque.

Curly Dryden won the Trophy with Norton power and Peter Collins was close behind in a similar car. John Cooper came third with his JAP-powered works Cooper, but J.R. Stoop prevented a clean sweep by driving his CFS-Special into fourth place. Ken Wharton came fifth in a Cooper-BSA and Eric Brandon, who had been a close third for much of the race, was sixth in his Cooper-JAP after a visit to the pits.

Another very enjoyable and exciting day spent in the heart of the Sussex countryside.

On 30th September 1950, one BRM with its original, sleek body was entered in two races driven by Reg Parnell. Like the Easter meeting, earlier in the year, the day was one of the few wet Goodwoods. Grey and overcast, it just drizzled for most of the day and at times, rained quite hard. A lot of umbrellas were to be seen in the crowd. In one sense it was quite miserable for the spectators, but it made the racing more exciting to watch as the track was

quite treacherous and must have been hard work for the drivers.

In the Woodcote Cup, Reg Parnell, from the front row of the grid, was in the lead at the end of the first lap and stayed there to the flag. B. Bira driving a Maserati 4CLT was in second place at the end of lap three after a fantastic drive from the back of the grid, and stayed there with Baron de Graffenried in a similar Maserati finishing third.

Reg Parnell also won the *Daily Graphic* Goodwood Trophy race in the BRM in much the same way, but from row three on the grid; once again Bira made a fantastic start in his Maserati and was in second place by the end of the first lap. It seemed that the rain made no difference to his driving at all. However, try as he might, he just could not catch the flying Reggie. The Baron again finished in third place and fourth was Bob Gerard in his faithful ERA R14B.

This meeting showed that both Parnell and Bira were masters of the art of driving at high speed in the rain.

As the cars made a dash for Madgwick at the start of these races, a great cloud of spray was sent up. How Bira managed to see the cars in front as he carved his way through the field we shall never know.

Looking through the gloom across towards the Lavant Straight from our position at Madgwick, we could not see the cars but knew where they were by the plumes of spray they sent up as they accelerated away from Lavant Corner.

Everyone went home that day very damp and with extremely muddy feet, but the rain had not dampened our spirits and we had witnessed some great motor racing. Generally speaking, the weather had little effect on the enthusiasm of the spectators.

This was the first meeting to which I had taken my youngest brother, Trevor, who was just 10½ at the time. In spite of the rather appalling conditions on his first visit, he became a true Goodwood enthusiast and still is.

Both of my younger brothers and sister joined me in cycling to Goodwood for the motor racing just as soon as they were old enough to manage the 12 mile round trip and all the excitement. In 1950 I met a very nice young lady called Frankie (Frances) and, from the 1951 season onwards she was converted, and would cycle with us to Goodwood. In 1955 we were married and attended meetings regularly. In August 1956 we bought our first car, a 1924 Trojan. It had been sitting in a barn for 27 years, so needed some restoration, but by Easter 1958 she was well run-in and transported us to the circuit in fine style. She was our everyday transport for many years and we lost count of how many times she visited Goodwood. Usually she would sit patiently in the car park while we watched the goings-on round the circuit, but on occasions, such as the 1963 International Veteran and Vintage Car

"I'm glad I'm not a driver today – they must be soaked"
*"But **they** haven't got muddy feet!"*

Rally, she was allowed inside and on to the hallowed tarmac to take part in the event.

For the Easter Meeting of 1951, Bira had got himself an OSCA. This, I believe, was produced by the Maserati brothers who, by now, had nothing to do with the Maserati Company. It had a V12 engine of 4470 cc mounted in a 4CLT chassis and was fitted with quite an elegant body, probably a modified 4CLT. He drove it in three events and had a very good day.

In the Chichester Cup, he finished third behind Reg Parnell driving his Maserati 4CLT and Brian Shaw-Taylor in ERA R9B. He then won the Richmond Trophy with Shaw-Taylor second and Duncan Hamilton third in ERA R5B. And in the Fourth Easter Handicap he finished fourth.

He drove the big OSCA again in the Festival of Britain Trophy race at the Whit-Monday meeting and won the first heat, but sadly the car suffered some sort of malfunction in the final.

Bira had an exciting driving style. He always looked calm and relaxed by his facial expression (impossible to see these days) but he obviously gave 100%. Whatever car he drove, it would twitch and slide on the corners, indicating that it was very near to the limit of its good nature. He was one of my favourite drivers. A great pity that we did not see more of him at Goodwood. G

J. Duncan Hamilton (on right)
Very successful driver at Goodwood in the 1950s in a variety of racing and sports cars, and very popular with the Goodwood crowd. Photo: Peter Dyer.

Easter 1952

Mike Hawthorn, 2-litre Cooper–Bristol. First, Lavant Cup (five-lap race for Formula 2 cars), first, Chichester Cup (six-lap race for Formula Libre cars), second, Richmond Trophy (12-lap race for Formula 1 cars). (Photographer unknown.)

Froilan Gonzalez, 4½ litre Thin Wall Special Ferrari. First, Richmond Trophy (12-lap race for Formula 1 cars), also fastest lap at 90.00 mph. (Photographer unknown.)

Stirling Moss, C-Type Jaguar. Fastest lap in the First Easter Handicap at 82.60 mph. (Photographer unknown.)

Geoff Duke, Aston Martin DB3. Third, First Easter Handicap. (Photographer unknown.)

Easter 1954

Les Leston signing his autograph for my brother, Trevor. You can see we came on our bicycles by Trevor's trouser clips.

Duncan Hamilton's C-Type Jaguar.

Tommy Sopwith's "Sphinx" which raced at Goodwood on a number of occasions. This car was powered by an Armstrong Siddeley Sapphire engine.

George Abecassis

The works HWM-Jaguar of George Abecassis. Event 2, The First Easter Handicap, five-laps for Sports Cars, Abecassis was scratch man and finished in fifth place having set the fastest lap at 83.88 mph, equal with Jimmy Stewart driving an Ecurie Ecosse Jaguar XK120C who won the race having had 10 seconds start over Abecassis.

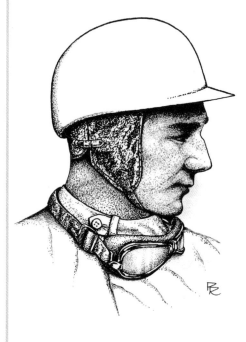

Stirling Moss
(now Sir Stirling Moss)

He was the most successful driver at Goodwood. From the first meeting in 1948 he was a winner. He drove cars of all types and sizes in every type of race held on this circuit and usually finished in the first three places. He was the winner of no less than 18 races in the period covered by this book. Often during the course of a meeting, he would compete in several quite different cars in different races and be equally successful with all of them. He must hold the record for the greatest number of different cars raced by one driver. His calm relaxed style of driving belied his speed, but by comparing his lap times with those of other drivers in the race it became obvious that he was the fastest on the track. Moss's overtaking skills, particularly when cornering, were a joy to watch. A master-class in precision driving. A race with Stirling Moss as one of the drivers was always great for the spectators.

Whit–Monday 14th May 1951
"500" International Trophy, Final, 15 laps.
Stirling Moss (Kieft-Norton), winner, at St Mary's.
Alan Brown (Cooper-Norton), second, David Clarke (Cooper-Norton), third.

Stirling Moss

Commer transporter
(with appropriate number)
Maserati 250F for the use of.

Stirling Moss (centre facing camera)
and the Francis Beart Cooper 500 photographed
at the Easter meeting 1954.

Stirling Moss
with his Standard road car (note
the registration number) with a
spot of wheel trouble.

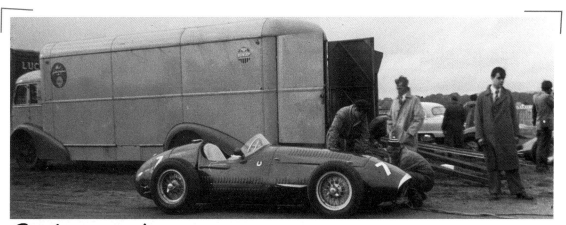

Stirling Moss' 250F Maserati and the Transporter/Workshop and mechanics from Officine Alfieri Maserati.

The 250F Maserati among some interesting machinery. Stirling Moss' Standard road car is in the foreground and car no. 17 (centre above and right below) is the Ecurie Ecosse Cooper-Bristol of P. Hughes.

September 1954 Stirling Moss in the works Maserati 250F through the chicane. Photo: Alan R. Smith.

The Best of British
Stirling Moss in the 1957 Vanwall
Photo: Alan R. Smith

Dr Giuseppe "Nino" Farina

It was great, in 1951, to see the first ever motor racing World Champion (1950) racing at Goodwood. His style was relaxed, yet awe inspiring. He seemed to be driving on the limit all the time, yet he managed to keep the car on the black stuff.

Sadly, for the spectators, he raced at only three Goodwood meetings but managed three wins with the Alfa Romeo 159, two second places with 4CLT Maseratis and a second place with the famous Thin Wall Special. A fantastic achievement from just three visits.

29th September 1951
Daily Graphic 15-lap Formula 1 race for the Goodwood Trophy.
Giuseppe Farina (Alfa Romeo), winner, at St Mary's.

Around the paddock

A rather splendid Bristol.

Nearly new Mercedes.

The Rolls Royce Silver Ghost about to take to the track.

Rolls Royce (left), Vintage Sunbeam (middle), and 30s Sunbeam (right).

Chapter 3

Four wheel drift! "Nino" Farina in the Alfa Romeo 158/9 on his way to win the Goodwood Trophy from Reg Parnell in the Thin Wall Special. September 1951.

International flavour

In those days, the camaraderie between drivers was obvious. Those who were entered to drive works cars would sometimes get other drivers to drive their own machines in the same race. Reg Parnell would do this regularly. I well remember Stirling Moss entering his own Maserati in a race to be driven by his friend and rival, Mike Hawthorn. Other drivers also drove this car on occasions. Sadly, those days are gone for ever, except in the realms of amateur, club racing. In the highly competitive, commercial world of Formula One today it really is completely different.

The Whit-Monday meeting of 1951 had a real Brooklands flavour. Races for the International Trophy, in two heats and a final for 500 cc racing cars and the *Daily Graphic* Festival of Britain Trophy took up the whole meeting. The Festival of Britain Trophy race was to Formula Libre. This meant cars, which complied with previous Grand Prix formula, but not the present one could race alongside those of the current Formula 1.

The heats were run over seven laps and the finals were 15 laps each. This was most exciting and kept the spectators on their toes all afternoon.

"...and he takes the chequered flag..."

"500" International Trophy

The 500 cc event went as follows:

Heat 1

1 Eric Brandon (Cooper V)

2 D.A. Clarke (Cooper V)

3 J.F. Westcott (JBS)

Heat 2

1 Alan Brown (Cooper V)

2 Bernie Ecclestone (Cooper V)

3 Ken McAlpine (JBS)

(Bernie Ecclestone—who's he?)

Final

1 Stirling Moss (Kieft)

2 Alan Brown (Cooper V)

3 D.A. Clarke (Cooper V)

The races for the Festival of Britain Trophy were absolutely fantastic, with a whole range of pre- and post-war cars competing together and with a truly international line up of drivers.

The cars included ERAs, Talbots, Maseratis, Alfa Romeos, Coopers, the Thin Wall Special, an Allard, a Darracq, and many more.

The racing was fast and furious and no quarter was given by anyone. The pre-war ERAs were lapping nearly as fast as the Thin Wall Special and the Maseratis.

Overtaking was not easy for anyone. Reg Parnell made a great start from pole position and lead from start to finish in Heat 1. The full result:

1 Reg Parnell (Thin Wall Special)

2 Baron de Graffenried (Maserati)

3 Brian Shaw-Taylor (ERA R8C)

4 Bob Gerard (ERA R4A)

5 J. Duncan Hamilton (Talbot)

6 Tony Rolt (ERA-Delage)

Heat 2 was just as exciting. From row three on the grid, Bira in the 12-cylinder four-and-a-half litre OSCA made a fantastic start and by the end of the first lap was in second place. By the end of lap two he was in the lead and stayed there. Dennis Poore in the big Alfa, also from row three, went with Bira and was in second place on laps two and three but was overtaken by Farina and then David Hampshire, both driving Maseratis.

1 B. Bira (OSCA)

2 Giuseppe Farina (Maserati)

3 David Hampshire (Maserati)

4 Dennis Poore (Alfa Romeo)

5 Johnny Claes (Talbot)

6 Harry Schell (Maserati)

The final was a culmination of the excitement from both heats rolled into one and although the lap chart may indicate a procession, the cars were so evenly matched and close together that the result was certainly not a for-gone conclusion. Result:

1 Reg Parnell (Thin Wall Special)

2 Giuseppe Farina (Maserati)

3 Baron de Graffenried (Maserati)

4 Brian Shaw-Taylor (ERA R8C)

5 J. Duncan Hamilton (Talbot)

6 Tony Rolt (ERA-Delage)

7 Johnny Claes (Talbot)

8 Graham Whitehead (ERA R10B)

When looking at the results of the September meeting of 1951, you might think that the entry list was small, but I can assure you that there were just as many cars and drivers there that day as usual. However, among the few names which appear in the results list, just two stand out: Giuseppe Farina and Stirling Moss. Moss, driving just two cars, won three races, was second in another and fifth in the final race of the day.

Farina drove just one car at this meeting, the beautiful Alfa Romeo 159. In the Formula Libre Woodcote Cup he beat Reg Parnell in the Thin Wall Special into second place. Third was Tony Rolt in the ERA-Delage. In the Third September Handicap, Farina drove the Alfa into first place ahead of Stirling Moss in the HWM-Alta with Reg Parnell third in the Thin Wall. Then Farina completed his Alfa hat trick by winning the Goodwood Trophy ahead of Reg Parnell (in the Thin Wall again) and Tony Rolt in the ERA-Delage.

Stirling Moss had a busy day, as usual, driving his two cars. As mentioned previously, he finished second in the Third September Handicap and fifth in the Goodwood Trophy driving the HWM-Alta. But he had started the day in Event 1, the Madgwick Cup, ahead of Lance Macklin and George Abecassis making it an HWM 1-2-3. Then he jumped into a C-Type Jaguar and won the five-lap sports car race ahead of David Clarke in a Frazer Nash and Hugh Howarth in an XK120, and the Second September Handicap beating Hugh Howarth's XK120 again with Philip Fotheringham-Parker's XK120 in third place.

I am sure that the drivers had enjoyed themselves, the spectators certainly had and once again it had been a really great day out at Beautiful Goodwood.

The Goodwood experience was made all the more enjoyable for the spectator by the excellent, very informative and often humorous commentary via the public address system by the likes of John Bolster, McDonald Hobley, James Tilling, and others. Handicap and long distance races would have been very hard to follow without it. Also, news of what was happening in the pits was a bonus. Very welcome and interesting background information about the drivers and cars was passed on to the spectators by these wonderful characters in their little glass commentary boxes.

At the September meeting of 1952, Stirling Moss had another busy day at the office, he drove the new, but ill-fated G-Type ERA in Event 1, The Madgwick Cup (Formula 2), Event 3, The Woodcote Cup (Formula Libre), and Event 7, The Goodwood Trophy, where he managed to encourage it into fifth place. Also, he drove his own 500 cc Cooper into first place in Event 2 and Tommy Wisdom's C-Type Jaguar into second place in Event 4.

At the September meeting of 1954 Stirling Moss and Roy Salvadori went off with most of the silverware between them as the results show:

Five-Lap Race for 500 cc Racing Cars
1 Don Parker (Kieft)
2 Stirling Moss (Cooper)

Five-Lap Sports Car Race A
1 Roy Salvadori (Maserati)
2 Stirling Moss (Lister-Bristol)
3 Alan Brown (Cooper-Bristol)

Goodwood Trophy. 21-Lap for GP Cars
1 Stirling Moss (Maserati)
2 Peter Collins (Vanwall)
3 Roy Salvadori (Maserati)

Five-Lap Sports Car Race B
1 Roy Salvadori (Jaguar XK120C)
2 Masten Gregory (Ferrari 4.5)
3 George Abecassis (HWM)

Woodcote Cup. Ten-Lap. Formula Libre
1 Peter Collins (Thin Wall Special)
2 Ken Wharton (BRM 16 cyl 1500)
3 Stirling Moss (Maserati)
4 Mike Hawthorn (Vanwall)
5 Roy Salvadori (Maserati)

At this meeting Roy Salvadori was driving the Gilby Engineering Maseratis as usual and the Ecurie Ecosse XK120C.

I believe that the Maserati 250F which was driven by Stirling Moss that day was his own, but that it had been prepared and entered by the Maserati works. G

Car no. 60 is the AC Ace of B.G.P. de Mattos in which he finished second in Event 6, the five-lap Handicap for non-supercharged sports cars. Presumably 60A was a practice car.

Reg Bicknell's unusual streamlined front end on his 497 cc Revis.

E.W. Holt driving Graham Whitehead's ERA R8B/C.

This, non-competing, 1933 Alfa Romeo Touring bodied "Le Mans" 8 cyl 2300 was first registered by Count Johnny Lurani and then exported to England to its first owner, famous Brooklands exponent, Lord Howe. It later passed to Home Kidson, brother of Glen Kidson, one of the Bentley boys, who used it as a race car before, during, and after the war, before trading it in for a Mercedes 300SL.

1064 cc Lotus of M.G.H. MacDowel who finished fifth in Event 6, five-lap Handicap for non-supercharged sports cars.

P. Jopp's Emeryson in which he finished sixth in Event 1, The Goodwood National "500", 15-lap scratch race for 500 cc cars. These cars were unusual in this class having the engine in front of the driver.

25th September 1954
Preparing for the start of the 21-lap, Formula 1 Goodwood Trophy Race. Louis Rosier on the fourth row of the grid in the Ecurie Louis Rosier 250F Maserati. Car number 26 is the Border Reivers' Cooper-Bristol of J.K. Hall. The car beside Rosier is believed to be the Ecurie Ecosse Cooper-Bristol of P. Hughes.
Photo: Alan R. Smith

Photo: Alan R. Smith

Peter Collins on the front row of the grid beside the Vanwall Special in which he finished second to Stirling Moss in the works 250F Maserati. Car no. 20 (behind the Vanwall Special) is Leslie Marr's Connaught. Later that day, Peter Collins, driving the Thin Wall Special Ferrari, won the ten-lap, Formula Libre Woodcote Cup ahead of Ken Wharton (V16 BRM), Stirling Moss (250F), and Mike Hawthorn, who had taken over the Vanwall Special.

John V. Bolster

A well-known racing driver pre-war, best remembered for his Bolster Special, "Bloody Mary", with which he mostly went hill climbing with great success. After the war he took to driving ERAs and drove R11B (entered by Reg Parnell) into third place in the race for racing cars over 1450 cc supercharged at Goodwood's first meeting in 1948.

However, it was his distinctive voice over the public address system for which he will be best remembered by the Goodwood spectators. With his clear, fruity voice and wonderful sense of humour, he kept us informed of everything that happened, as it happened, in the pit area both before and during the races.

On practice days he would be seen strolling round the paddock in his striking deer-stalker and sports jacket, chatting with drivers and mechanics and having many a passing merry quip with us, the public. Truly, one of the great characters of the motor racing scene at that time.

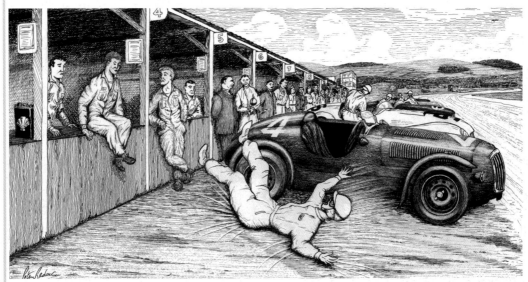

"I told him not to wear those shoes for a Le Mans start"

Chapter 4

Goodwood 18th April 1949. Richmond Trophy ten-lap race to Formula 1—Madgwick corner. Bob Gerard in his ERA R14B being followed by Kenneth McAlpine driving the ex-Whitney Straight, ex-Bira 2.9 litre Maserati and another ERA, believed to be R9B driven by G.E. Ansell.

The ERA era

In the early days of the Goodwood Motor Circuit, ERA cars had great success and, from a spectator point of view, they were great to watch; especially when driven by the likes of Bob Gerard, Brian Shaw-Taylor, and Graham Whitehead.

A number of other people drove ERAs, among them one John Bolster, whose distinctive voice was to become part of the Goodwood experience with his unique style of commentating, usually from the pit area.

At the first ever meeting, in September 1948 when Reg Parnell won the Goodwood Trophy in his Maserati 4CLT, ERAs took five of the next seven places:

1 Reg Parnell (Maserati 4CLT)
2 Bob Gerard (ERA R14B)
3 David Hampshire (ERA R1A)
4 Cuth Harrison (ERA R8C)
5 Duncan Hamilton (Maserati 6CM)
6 Geoffrey Ansell (ERA R9B)
8 Peter Walker (ERA R7B)

The previous race, for racing cars over 1450cc s/c was won by Dennis Poore in his Alfa Romeo.

Whit–Saturday 27th May 1950
1st Whitsun Handicap, five laps, Madgwick.
Tony Rolt driving Rob Walker's ERA-Delage finished in third place behind
the MGs of de Lisa and Haesendonck who had 1½ minutes start.

But there were ERAs close behind. Peter Walker finished second in R7B and John Bolster was third in R11B. Three other ERAs were in that race also.

At the Easter meeting 1949, ERAs were again close behind Reg Parnell's Maserati when he won the Richmond Trophy. Second was Peter Whitehead in R10B, third, Cuth Harrison in R8C and in fifth place was Leslie Johnson in GP2. That year Bob Gerard won the British Grand Prix at Silverstone in ERA R14B. A combination often seen at Goodwood.

At the September meeting 1949, ERAs finished second and third in the Woodcote Cup.

At the Easter meeting 1950, ERAs finished third and fourth in the Richmond Trophy and sixth, eighth, and tenth in the Third Easter Handicap. In May, Shaw-Taylor brought home R9B in fourth place in the Whitsun Handicap and at the September meeting, ERAs finished in two third places, two fourth places and a fifth.

Easter 1951 saw five ERAs entered in the Chichester Cup. Shaw-Taylor in R9B came in second, Bob Gerard in R14B was fourth and Graham Whitehead was sixth in R10B.

ERAs finished second and third in the Second Easter Handicap and second and third again plus seventh in the Richmond Trophy. They made a day of it by being fourth and fifth in the Fourth Easter Handicap.

The Festival of Britain Trophy race at the Whit-Monday Meeting that year where they did well has been covered already, but ERAs went on to score many more places at Goodwood meetings over the next few years until they were out classed by the coming of the Maserati 250F and the Cooper-Bristol and Lotus cars. It was these two makes which started the trend to put the engine behind the driver and this, sadly, marked the end of an era.

F.R. "Bob" Gerard

Always an exciting driver to watch, from day one a regular competitor at Goodwood. At the first meeting he finished second in the Goodwood Trophy race for Formula 1 cars behind Reg Parnell's 4CLT Maserati driving his elderly ERA. He regularly raced his ERAs into the early 1950s and usually finished in the first three places.
In 1951 he won his heat and the final of the 500 International driving his Cooper-Norton. Over the following few years he had many successes with his Cooper-Bristol.

In two of the Goodwood Nine-hour races, Gerard entered and drove his Le-Mans Replica Frazer Nash with co-driver David Clarke. In 1952 they finished fourth and in 1953 they finished in sixth place. The spectators were always pleased to see his name in the programme.

17th September 1949, 10-lap Goodwood Trophy Race
Bob Gerard in his ERA R14B finished third behind Parnell's Maserati and Walker's E-Type ERA. This is the same car as that shown on page 31 but with a new nose and front axle following a coming together with Tony Rolt's Alfa Romeo in that race.

It is quite remarkable and, I believe, unique in motor racing, that cars built in the mid- to late-1930s were still competitive to such a degree at race meetings all over the British Isles and in Europe some 15 years later.

ERA R5B was seen racing at Goodwood many times, in the hands of several different drivers. Ordered by the White Mouse Stable in October 1935 for Bira to drive and called Remus (a partner to Romulus—R2B) it was to become the most raced racing car of all time. Originally fitted with a 1500 cc engine, it was raced by Bira in 1936 but afterwards used mainly as a source of spares for Romulus. It was bought and raced by Tony Rolt in 1938 and 1939.

After the war, it was bought by Ian Connell and over the next few years it was raced by several people, including John Bolster, Duncan Hamilton, and Philip Fotheringham-Parker. In 1956 it was bought by Bill Moss and raced extensively by him until the end of 1958 when the Hon. Patrick Lindsay bought it. He raced it at five or six meetings each year. In 1979 it raced at 13 meetings including Donington, Silverstone, Thruxton, Oulton Park, and Monaco. For the Grand Prix meeting at Silverstone it was fitted with a brand new two-litre engine. Since Patrick Lindsay's untimely death, this car has been raced regularly by his son, Ludovic, and no doubt will continue to be for many years to come. G

George: Have you got any spare plugs?

Fred: Yes. Do you want six?

George: No. Just two.

Fred: Why only two? It's a six cylinder, isn't it?

George: *Ear* plugs!
They've put us next to the BRMs.

"B. Bira"
Prince Birabongse
of Siam

This very popular driver had been very successful in the 1930s, especially with the ERAs, which he drove in the striking blue and yellow colours of his native Siam. Also in those days he had driven, among other cars, the ex Whitney Straight 2.9 litre straight-eight Maserati which was raced at Goodwood by Kenneth McAlpine and H.C. Spero.

Bira raced at Goodwood only a few times in the early 1950s but gave great pleasure to the spectators with his 4CLT Maserati with which he achieved one win, two second places, and a third. Then, with the big four-and-a-half litre OSCA he had two wins and two third places. Quite a spectacular driver to watch, he seemed to have no fear and appeared to take corners at the same speed as the straights.

Easter Monday 26th March 1951
Richmond Trophy, 12-lap race for Formula 1 cars.
"B. Bira" (OSCA G-4500), winner, at Woodcote. Brian Shaw-Taylor (ERA R9B), second, J. Duncan Hamilton (ERA R5B), third. New lap record by "B. Bira" (OSCA) at 90.38 mph.

Easter Monday 19th April 1954
Lavant Cup, seven-lap Formula 1 race.
Reg Parnell (Ferrari 500), first, Roy Salvadori (Maserati 250F), second at Fordwater.

Mike Hawthorn (in cap) with interesting machinery in the background.

Chapter 5

Just visiting! Mike Couper's Armstrong Siddeley Sapphire.
This car had won the "Prix d'Honour" at the Monte Carlo Rally.

Ambience

On practice and race days at Goodwood the car parks would be filled with pre-war vehicles and it was well worth spending time wandering round them. Among the Austin, Morris, Ford, and Standard brigade would be found a generous scattering of Bentleys, Bugattis, Sunbeams, and Alvises (or should that be Alvii). Sometimes we would spot the more exotic such as Hispano-Suiza, Alfa Romeo, OM, or Crossley.

When racing had finished, we would sometimes linger a while on the verge of one of the roads leading from the car parks and watch the cavalcade of interesting machinery slowly making its way to the main road.

For the spectator, part of the appeal of Goodwood was that during the course of a race meeting, some drivers would compete in several races in several different cars. Stirling Moss and Roy Salvadori were masters of this art as browsing through my collection of Goodwood programmes shows only too clearly.

For example, the meeting on Easter Monday 1955 saw Roy Salvadori on top form. The results were as follows:

Event 1 Lavant Cup—Formula 2

1 Roy Salvadori (Connaught A)

2 Bob Gerard (Cooper-Bristol)

3 Don Beauman (Connaught A)

Event 3 Chichester Cup—Formula Libre

1 Peter Collins (BRM P30 Mk2)

2 Roy Salvadori (Maserati 250F)

3 Stirling Moss (Maserati 250F)

Event 5 Sports Car Race—over 2000 cc

1 Roy Salvadori (Aston Martin DB3S)

2 Mike Sparken (Ferrari 750 Monza)

3 Duncan Hamilton (Jaguar D-Type)

Event 7 Richmond Trophy—Formula 1

1 Roy Salvadori (Maserati 250F)

2 Bob Gerard (Cooper-Bristol T23)

3 Don Beauman (Connaught A)

Event 8 Easter Handicap—Five Laps

1 Bob Gerard (Cooper-Bristol T23)

2 Roy Salvadori (Maserati 250F)

3 John Young (Connaught A)

Salvadori also finished fourth in Event 2, the sports car race for up to 1500 cc cars driving a Cooper-Maserati.

The excitement which I felt that day as we witnessed the immense talent of this relatively young man is with me to this day whenever I think about it. Just to take an active part in six out of eight races in a short space of time that afternoon, in four very different cars, was quite a feat in itself. But to win three of those, come second in two more, and finish fourth in the other is almost beyond belief.

I was already a fan of Roy Salvadori, but from that day on he was a hero.

Our favourite vantage-point on the circuit was about half way round Madgwick corner. From here, when we stood on the mound, we could see the start and finish area, the whole of Madgwick and well down Fordwater. Also, we could catch a glimpse across the airfield of the cars as they sped down the Lavant Straight.

In the distance, overlooking the circuit from the north is the Trundle. This is the imposing hill just to the west of the famous Goodwood horse Race Course. As a schoolboy, during the war years and just after, I spent many happy hours on my bicycle in the lanes around this part of West Sussex and on occasions would attempt the long slog up the hill to the Race Course. Sometimes, if I had enough energy left, I would abandon my bike and scramble to the top of the Trundle.

From here there is a 360 degree view of West Sussex, East Hampshire, and beyond. On a clear day it is possible to see the Isle of Wight to the south-west, beyond and a little to the right of, the imposing spire of Chichester Cathedral. To the south-east stands Bognor gas-works, like a giant pepper-pot.

It is like looking at a three-dimensional map. There before me, all those years ago, was the Westhampnett airfield. Little did I know that one day I would be down there, as a witness to some very exciting motor racing. I remember seeing aircraft on the ground but I don't recall ever seeing one take off or land while I was up there almost in the clouds. Perhaps they knew that I was there, watching.

Juan-Manuel Fangio

In my humble opinion, the world's greatest Grand Prix racing driver of all time, Michael Schumacher included. The way in which Fangio won the 1957 German Grand Prix is just one of many examples why I think so.

Very sadly, for the spectators, he raced only twice at Goodwood. At the Easter meeting of 1952 he drove a rather "off song" Cooper-Bristol in the Chichester Cup race and managed to coax it into sixth place. And at the September meeting in 1953 he finished second in a V16 BRM behind a flying Mike Hawthorn in the Thin Wall Special in the Woodcote Cup. I saw him race, I have seen films of him racing, I have read all the reports of his achievements in motor racing and I have read what his racing driver contemporaries wrote about him. That is why I maintain that he is, without doubt, the World Number One Grand Prix driver of all time.

Easter Monday 14th April 1952
Chichester Cup, six-lap Formula Libre race.
Juan-Manuel Fangio (Cooper–Bristol), sixth at Fordwater.
Mike Hawthorn (Cooper–Bristol), winner, Tony Rolt (ERA–Delage), second.

Woodcote Cup five-lap race to Formula Libre—St Mary's. Mike Hawthorn driving the Thin Wall Special Ferrari to win, closely pursued by Juan-Manuel Fangio in the V16 BRM who finished second. Third was Ken Wharton in the second BRM.

I do, however, remember that on one occasion, I believe that it was during the summer following D-Day, in the distance I saw a group of Spitfires coming up from nearby Tangmere. They were heading west and as I watched, they banked left, flew out over the Solent and disappeared into the blue over the English Channel. What lay ahead for them that day I shall never know. A very emotional sight, which made me proud to be British.

Variety is everything

For the Easter Monday meetings, practice day was the Saturday and on those occasions the public was allowed into the paddock. We could get very close to those wonderful racing machines and watch the mechanics working on them. Sometimes the drivers would lend a hand, quite willing to get their hands dirty. We could peer into the backs of the transporters at all the spare parts and tools. We could rub shoulders with famous drivers (or should that be elbows). Everything was wonderfully informal and, in quite a different way, just as enjoyable as race day.

Between National and International events, the BARC would hold Members' Meetings. These were not open to the public but we used to cycle up to the circuit anyway and watch from behind the hedge on Madgwick or through a gateway on the Lavant Straight.

On one occasion, Frankie and I had just arrived near the track and were debating as to whether to stay near Madgwick or to go round to the Lavant straight, when a couple, who had just come out of the car park and were walking towards the circuit entrance called out to us. "Would you like some tickets?" It seemed that some friends of theirs, who were going to accompany them to the meeting, were unable to come, so they offered the spare tickets to us. Needless to say we were delighted to accept and could not thank them enough. We had a most enjoyable day.

As mentioned before, Madgwick corner was our favourite vantage point. Exciting things would happen here from time to time. On one occasion, Mike Hawthorn, driving a BRM, lost control and on exiting the corner, went high-speed grass cutting. The car did a somersault several feet in the air and Mike was thrown out on to the ground.

This was just as well as the car ended up with wheels skywards. Mike got up quite casually, dusted himself down and strolled off towards the paddock, seemingly shaken but not stirred. The cause was mechanical failure and not driver error, I hasten to add.

On another occasion, Froilan Gonzalez, I believe in an early version of the Thin Wall Special, while trying to overtake another car on the outside at Madgwick, slid on to the grass and ended up almost at right angles

to the track. He let in the clutch while the engine revs were at near maximum and showered the spectators with grass cuttings. He rejoined the track at such speed that he went straight off the other side. He still managed to avoid stalling his engine, rejoined the track once more and tore off towards Fordwater, engine roaring, in a cloud of dust.

Also at this point, 500 cc cars often had arguments with the straw bales, particularly just after the start of a race. Invariably the cars came off second best. Usually the driver would climb out of the car, relatively unhurt but with a disgusted look on his face and climb over the straw bales out of harm's way. Just occasionally the driver would suffer some serious damage as well as the car. Motor racing is a dangerous sport!

We enjoyed our times at Madgwick so much that when we bought our first house we called it "Madgwick" and when we moved to our present one, we brought the name with us. This is appropriate in the sense that we are on

"I think the transmission's gone"

a corner, however, without all the noise and excitement.

Sports cars seemed especially prone to spinning at Madgwick, particularly on wet days. Some of the more exuberant drivers would approach the corner too fast or, perhaps, on the wrong line, the tail would break away and suddenly they would be facing the wrong way with the rest of the field passing them (with any luck) at speed on both sides. Sometime they would end up on the grass after practising the waltz, then simply spin the car round, rejoin the track, and set off in pursuit of the rest of the field playing tail end Charley.

There are some interesting facts to be found by looking through the 1950s Goodwood Programmes. I found that Colin Chapman, as well as competing with not a little success driving his brain-child "Lotus" cars, also drove an Emeryson on at least one occasion.

The programme for the autumn meeting of 1951 shows that in the first September Handicap, a certain J.M. Hawthorn was entered to drive a 1500 cc Riley entered by his father.

At the same meeting in the race for the Madgwick Cup, HWM cars finished first,

Lance Macklin (1954 2½ litre HWM).

J.M. "Mike" Hawthorn

Britain's first F1 World Champion won six races and finished second in three others in just six years racing at Goodwood. The first race he won at this circuit was the Formula 2 Lavant Cup at the 1952 Easter Monday meeting. Also that day, with the same car, his Cooper-Bristol T20, he won the Formula Libre Chichester Cup and finished second in the Formula 1 Richmond Trophy race. At the Whitsun meeting a few weeks later, he won the Sussex International Trophy (Formula Libre) again driving the Cooper.

At the September meeting in 1953 he won both the Woodcote Cup and the Goodwood Trophy driving the Thin Wall Special and at the Whitsun meeting in 1954 he finished second twice driving a Lotus-Climax 11.

In 1958 he won the Glover Trophy driving a Ferrari Dino 246.

26th September 1953
Goodwood Trophy, 15-lap Formula Libre race, Woodcote.
Mike Hawthorn (Thin Wall Special), first, Ken Wharton (V16 BRM), second.

second, and third in the hands of Stirling Moss, Lance Macklin, and George Abecassis.

Remembering this meeting and referring to my programme again, the Third September Handicap saw a great piece of driving by Giuseppe Farina in an Alfa Romeo 159. He was scratch man in a five-lap race in a field of 13 cars. First away was Gerry Dunham in his two-and-a-half litre Alvis, a full 60 seconds ahead. By the end of lap one, Farina was in eleventh place. By the end of lap two he was ninth. Lap three, sixth, lap four, fourth, and he took the lead from a young Stirling Moss on the last lap to win the race.

Stirling Moss gave a quality display in this race also. He had just 47 seconds start on the great Farina and in the first lap had overhauled all those in front of him and finished the lap leading the race. He stayed in the lead until Farina passed him in the closing stages of the last lap.

Farina's fastest lap in this race was 96.92 mph. With the same car later in the day he won the Goodwood Trophy at an average speed of 95.11 mph and put in a lap of 97.11 mph. Some going on such a small, and twisty, circuit.

Result:

1 Farina (Alfa Romeo s/c 1488 cc)
2 Parnell (Thin Wall Special 4500 cc)
3 Rolt (Delage s/c 1496 cc)
4 Gerard (ERA s/c 1488 cc)
5 Moss (HWM 1960 cc)

Five different makes of car in the first five, two of them dating from pre-war.

Headlights needed

1952 saw the first Nine-hour race at Goodwood. This really was a spectacle, starting at 3.00 pm and finishing at midnight. This was the first time for many of us to witness motor racing in the dark. Once again we were at Madgwick corner and enjoyed every minute of it. The drama heightened when fire broke out in the Aston Martin pits when the Reg Parnell/Eric Thompson DB3 was being refuelled. Fortunately nobody was seriously hurt and the race continued.

After dark, the headlights of the cars, as they sped down the start and finish straight, nearly blinded us. The brake discs would glow as they approached the corner and, with the constant pit stops, it was difficult to keep track of race positions. Thank goodness for an excellent commentary.

Again I find it interesting that there were five different makes of car in the first six places at the finish of the race:

1 Peter Collins/Pat Griffiths (Aston Martin DB3)
2 Tom Cole/Peter Whitehead (Ferrari 225)
3 Bobby Baird/Roy Salvadori (Ferrari 225)
4 Bob Gerard/David Clarke (Frazer Nash LMR)
5 Stirling Moss/Peter Walker (Jaguar C-Type)
6 Jim Mayers/Mike Keen (Lester MG) G

The incredible V16 BRM in the paddock at Goodwood, September 1952. This car was driven by J.F. Gonzalez to win both the five-lap Woodcote Cup and the 15-Lap *Daily Graphic* Goodwood Trophy. Photo: Peter Dyer.

The V16 years

Over the three years 1952–4 the sometimes rather maligned V16 BRM had very successful outings at Goodwood. I thought that they were wonderful machines and still do. They were unreliable in the early days and maybe they were not up to staying the distance of a full Grand Prix. Also, by all accounts, they were difficult to handle: **but that sound!!! And all that power!!!** And in the hands of Reg Parnell, Ken Wharton, and Froilan Gonzalez they were a joy to watch.

In the 1952 five-lap, Formula Libre, Woodcote Cup, Froilan Gonzalez in his machine lead from start to finish. Reg Parnell in the second BRM started a good second but was overtaken by Giuseppe Farina in the Thin Wall Special and finished third.

Later that day in the Goodwood Trophy (15 laps to Formula Libre), once again Froilan Gonzalez lead from start to finish. Reg Parnell and Ken Wharton made it a BRM 1-2-3.

At the Easter meeting of 1953 there were two BRMs in the Chichester Cup Race (five laps to Formula Libre). Baron de Graffenried won the race in his Maserati A6GCM, but Ken Wharton finished second in his BRM and Reg Parnell came in fourth in his. Third place was remarkably taken by Ron Flockhart in his pre-war ERA.

Later in the day Ken Wharton and his BRM won the Glover Trophy 15-lap race.

1 Ken Wharton (BRM V16)
2 Piero Taruffi (Thin Wall Special)
3 de Graffenried (Maserati A6GCM)
4 Roy Salvadori (Connaught)
5 Tony Rolt (Connaught)
6 Bob Gerard (Cooper-Bristol)
7 Ron Flockhart (ERA R4D)

This sort of racing really was great to watch because of the variety of cars all in one race. Clearly, the ERAs and Cooper-Bristols were unlikely to win unless the more powerful machines had problems, but we spectators were amazed just how close the racing was and at the finish of the race above, Flockhart's pre-war, ex Raymond Mays ERA really wasn't that far behind. This is what made a day at Goodwood truly great.

At the September meeting of 1953, the Woodcote Cup was won by Mike Hawthorn driving the Thin Wall Special, but the Maestro himself, Juan-Manuel Fangio, finished second in a V16 BRM, and third was Ken Wharton in

the second BRM. Stirling Moss came home fourth in the Cooper-Alta, fifth was Bob Gerard in his Cooper-Bristol, and sixth was G.N. Richardson driving his ERA.

Mike Hawthorn also won the Goodwood Trophy race driving the Thin Wall later that day and Ken Wharton finished second in the BRM. Third home was Bob Gerard driving his Cooper-Bristol.

The Easter Monday meeting of 1954 saw Ron Flockhart and Ken Wharton driving two V16 BRMs. Flockhart's driving of his old ERA the previous year had obviously impressed the BRM management. The Chichester Cup was won by Ken Wharton with Ron Flockhart finishing fourth. In second place was Roy Salvadori in the Gilby Engineering Maserati 250F and third was Reg Parnell driving a Ferrari 500/625.

Ken Wharton won the Glover Trophy also that day in the BRM and again Ron Flockhart came fourth. Second was Ken McAlpine and third Leslie Marr both driving Connaughts.

The 1954 Whit Monday meeting the Whitsun Trophy race, over 15 laps to Formula Libre, finished thus:

1 Peter Collins (Thin Wall Special)
2 Ron Flockhart (V16 BRM)
3 Roy Salvadori (Maserati 250F)
4 Ken Wharton (V16 BRM)

The September meeting that year was, what I believe to be, the last outing for the V16 BRMs, at least "in anger" as they say. The Woodcote Cup was won once again by the Thin Wall Special being driven by Peter Collins. Ken Wharton managed to bring the sole BRM in the race into second place. Stirling Moss was third in a works-entered 250F Maserati and Mike Hawthorn came home fourth in a Vanwall. G

Jose Froilan "Pepito" Gonzalez

Also known as the "Pampas Bull", Gonzalez raced at only two Goodwood meetings but left a lasting impression on all those who saw him drive a racing car. At the Easter meeting of 1952 he drove the Ferrari Thin Wall Special, in its early form, into first place in the Formula 1 race for the Richmond Trophy.

He returned to the circuit for the September meeting when he drove the V16 BRM in two events and won both. The Formula Libre Woodcote Cup, when Giuseppe Farina finished second in the updated Thin Wall Special and Reg Parnell third in another BRM, and the *Daily Graphic* Goodwood Trophy when Reg Parnell and Ken Wharton made it a BRM 1-2-3. His exuberant and aggressive style was great to watch, such a shame that he did not drive more often at Goodwood.

27th September 1952 Woodcote Cup, five-lap Formula Libre race
Froilan Gonzalez (V16 BRM), first at Madgwick.
Giuseppe Farina (Thin Wall Special), second, Reg Parnell (V16 BRM), third.

25th September 1954
The 21-lap, Formula 1 Goodwood Trophy. The winner, Stirling Moss in his Maserati 250F through the chicane.

Joe Kelly's Ferrari 3 litre.
In Event 5, five-lap scratch race for non-supercharged sports cars of unlimited engine capacity, after being second by the end of lap three and recording the fastest lap of the race, the engine suffered some sort of mechanical failure and was retired from the race.

E.N. Whiteaway's HWM
The Paddock in September 1954.

September 1954

Graham Whitehead's Aston Martin DB3S.

This 2 litre Connaught entered by the Roebuck Engineering Co. and driven by M.F. Young finished sixth in the seven-lap Madgwick Cup.

The IER Midget of Ian Raby. In the five-lap scratch race for 500 cc cars, it left the road backwards at St Mary's and after a lengthy excursion, returned to the track and finished the race.

Anglo-American Rally 1954

1906 Wolseley–Siddeley

Rolls Royces of 1911 and 1927

1907 Rover and another Rolls Royce

1912 Sunbeam and a Renault

1913 Daimler

1913 Unic

50

Chapter 7

Two rather different Rolls Royces at the Anglo American rally of 1954.
On the left from 1911 and on the right from 1926.

Vintage and celebrities

In June 1954 the Goodwood Motor circuit saw some motor cars of a very different kind. It played host to The Anglo–American Veteran and Vintage Car Rally and Concours d'Elegance.

Looking through the photographs which I took that day with my very simple camera, I see that there was real variety among the entrants.

From a 1903 Gladiator to an enormous 1911 Rolls Royce limousine; a very pretty little 1913 Unic fixed head coupe to a giant Wolseley-Siddeley. A very desirable 1926 Rolls Royce drop head coupe with dickey seat and

quite a selection of Daimlers. Most makers of the period were represented.

It was a rather dull day as I recall, but it was dry and it was great to see so many beautiful early motor cars in such marvellous condition, which by 1954 were normally only seen at vintage events such as this; regrettably we see even less of them today.

Before moving on to the second half of the 1950s, a few thoughts on foreign drivers who competed at Goodwood.

I wish to take away nothing from the many great, as well as the lesser known, British drivers who thrilled us repeatedly over the years from 1948 to 1966 with their skills and dedication. But the spectators would always scan the programme to see who were the drivers from overseas at this meeting.

Giuseppe Farina, Froilan Gonzalez, the legendary Juan-Manuel Fangio, Baron de Graffenried, B. Bira, Louis Rosier, and others. Also, of course the great Jack Brabham, the talented Bruce McLaren, Jo Bonnier, Johnny Claes, Harry Schell from across the pond. All of these and others have raced at Goodwood and made the meetings that much more exciting.

The Easter meeting of 1955 (Salvadori day, pp. 55–56) saw the first outing (I believe) at Goodwood of the streamlined Connaught single-seater with all enveloping body. It looked beautiful, but seemed to be suffering from a few teething troubles.

The Whitsun meeting started with three sports car events for three different classes of cars. However, the meeting had a very different flavour to it. Event 4 was a five-lap Handicap for vintage cars. With a good selection of makes, it was wonderful and though the speed of these cars may not quite have matched that of the more modern machinery, they were just as exciting to watch. First away was Sir Francis Samuelson in his well-known 1914 Sunbeam. A few cars later, the circuit was full of Bentleys, Vauxhalls, an Amilcar, Bugatti, Riley, Alfa Romeo, etc.

The race was won by J. Tozer driving a pretty little 1927 Amilcar. Second was Jack Sears in his 1914 Sunbeam and third was G.G. McDonald in his 1927 four-and-a-half litre Bentley. It was really great to watch.

After the excitement of the vintage race, Event 5 was a five-lap Handicap race for lady drivers. This brought together a variety of cars and a good line up of drivers, most of whom were familiar names in motor sport.

"Remember it's got rather a fierce clutch"

My programme shows that there was a bit of re-arrangement in the order of departure between the printing and the event. Miss Hazel Dunham became "scratch", driving her father's AC and first away was Miss Rosemary Seers driving a TD MG.

Mrs Nancy Mitchell, who had 30 seconds start over Miss Dunham won the event in her Daimler. However, perhaps the handicappers were right as Miss Dunham came home a very close second after a fantastic drive through the field, no holds barred and putting in the fastest lap in the process at 71.29 mph. Third place went to Mrs Jean Bloxham driving the Ecurie Gordon White Aston Martin DB2 and fourth was Miss Betty Haig in her AC.

"Follow that!" might have been shouted, and it was. Event 6 was a Celebrities three-lap Handicap. Eight well-known personalities had been invited to race in their everyday cars and the list of starters and the handicapping makes interesting reading:

Ramond Baxter (Ford, 0.00)
Brian Reece (Sunbeam Talbot, 0.09)
Jon Pertwee (DKW, 0.12)
D. McDonald Hobley (Ford, 0.24)
Chris Brasher (Jowett, 0.24)
Lou Preager (Ford, 0.50)
John Gregson (Hillman, 1.00)
Richard Murdoch (Rolls Royce, 1.30)

The handicappers appreciated neither the speed and handling capabilities of a 1938 20/25 nor the driving skills of a radio comedian. Richard Murdoch fairly tore round the circuit and kept his elderly "Pride and Joy" in front right to the flag. Chris Brasher brought his Jowett Javelin in second with Brian Reece and Jon Pertwee close behind. Brian Reece made the fastest lap in his Sunbeam Talbot at 62.07 mph.

A real fun event which, I am sure, the drivers enjoyed just as much as the spectators.

The afternoon was rounded off by a 21-lap race for sports cars: the fastest from the first three races of the day. I believe that there were 28 cars, which formed up for a Le Mans type start. Quite a selection: D-Type, C-Type, XK120, HWM, Connaught, Cooper, Lotus, Aston Martin, Frazer Nash, Austin Healey, Lister, AC, and more.

It was fantastic when the flag dropped and all the drivers ran headlong across the track and jumped into their cars. The scramble to be first into Madgwick was not as bad as after a normal start. This was no doubt due to some drivers taking longer to get into their cars and get them started. But the sight of so many cars, nose to tail and side by side, at speed through Madgwick to Fordwater was quite unforgettable. The surface of the track could hardly be seen for cars. Needless to say, it was a long and exciting race during which a number of cars retired for a variety of reasons. However, it was nice to see some of the smaller cars up with the big boys at the finish.

1 Duncan Hamilton (D-Type)
2 Bob Berry (D-Type)
3 M. Anthony (Lotus-Bristol)
4 Tony Brooks (Frazer Nash)
5 Ken McAlpine (Connaught)
6 Peter Blond (Jaguar C-Type)

The fastest lap was recorded by Duncan Hamilton at 86.22 mph.

20th August 1955 was the date of the third and final Nine-hour race at Goodwood. I must

20th August 1955, Nine-hour race, St Mary's
Jaguar D-Type of Desmond Titterington and Ninian Sanderson.
This car finished in second place behind the winning Aston Martin DB3S driven by Peter Walker and
Dennis Poore.

say that I was sorry that there were no more. Watching the cars with their lights ablaze as darkness fell over the circuit was an entirely different experience to the other events we could see in this country and I believe that variety of events is what many spectators wanted. But not many enough, it seemed.

However, this race was just as exciting as the two previous ones. All the usual makes of car were there: Aston Martin, Jaguar, Ferrari, Lotus, Cooper, and Stirling Moss was driving a Porsche 550 Spyder with Huscke von Hanstein as co-driver.

There were a lot of accidents and retirements in the early stages of the race and when the Jaguar D-Type of Titterington and Sanderson was in first place it struck some markers, broke a headlight and lost vital time having it repaired. As darkness fell the Collins/Brooks Aston Martin was leading but this car also had some problems and spent time in the pits. The Aston Martin DB3S of Walker and Poore was leading as the minutes ticked away towards midnight and they had some gearbox problems to worry about. The Jaguar of Sanderson and Titterington was catching them fast but the clock struck twelve just in time to give Aston Martin its third Nine-hour victory. In third place was the Collins/Brooks DB3S. G

Roy Salvadori

11th April 1955 was Roy Salvadori day.

He was entered in six of the eight events. Results:

Lavant Cup: first, Connaught "A"

Chichester Cup: second, Maserati 250F

Sports Car Race "B": first, Aston Martin DB3S

Sports Car Race "C": fourth, Cooper-Maserati

Richmond Trophy: first, Maserati 250F

Easter Handicap: second, Maserati 250F

Roy Salvadori talking to Cliff Davis (sun glasses and moustache).

One of Salvadori's regular mounts, the Gilby Engineering Co.'s Maserati 250F. In the background is the Aston Martin DB3S which Peter Collins drove into fifth place in the five-lap over 2000 cc Sports Car race, which was won by Roy Salvadori driving the Gilby entered DB3S.

Roy Salvadori about to leave the Pits in the 250F Maserati, to put in a few practice laps.

The works Cooper-Climax which Salvadori drove at the September meeting 1956 to win both the 10-lap Woodcote Cup and the 10-lap Sussex Trophy. Notice the Cooper Co.'s Ford van behind.

Roy Salvadori

A very close second to Stirling Moss in the success table and in almost as many different cars, and Salvadori did not race at Goodwood until 1952. Often team mate to Moss and sometimes co-driver, he was as fast as he was successful. He always drove at 100% and at times left the spectators breathless just watching him.

Also, like Moss, he would jump from one car to another in successive races during a meeting and seem to have no difficulty in making each one go just as fast as the others.

In eight years he won 12 events at Goodwood, came second 12 times and finished in third place six times. His regular mounts were 250F Maserati, Cooper-Climax, and Aston Martin, but he drove Connaught also and several other makes over the years. A driver possessing great talent and a favourite with the spectators.

Easter Monday 11th April 1955
Lavant Cup, seven-lap Formula 2 race, Madgwick.
Roy Salvadori (Connaught "A"), winner. Bob Gerard (Cooper-Bristol), second.

The New Streamlined Connaught

This very striking car appeared for the first time at the Easter meeting 1955 driven by Tony Rolt. He finished fourth in the Formula Libre Chichester Cup, but retired from the Formula 1 Richmond Trophy.

These photos were taken on practice day.

Easter 1955. Bob Gerard (centre, wearing jumper) with his wife, Joan (second from right), with others, perhaps inspecting a broken piece of machinery or maybe having a quick snack between practice sessions. Below, his Cooper-Bristol and mechanics photographed at the September 1954 meeting. At that meeting, driving this car, Gerard won the Madgwick Cup (seven-lap scratch race for non-supercharged racing cars up to 2000 cc), he finished fourth in the Goodwood Trophy (21-laps for cars up to Grand Prix Formula) and sixth in the Woodcote Cup (Formula Libre ten-lap scratch race).

Bob Gerard's cars, particularly his famous ERA R14B, as well as being meticulously prepared mechanically, were always beautifully turned out when they appeared at race meetings. With bodywork painted in bright green and wheels in yellow they were very distinctive and easily recognised from a distance as he sped round the circuit. After covering many laps of the circuit on practice day and becoming very dusty and sometimes wet, the car would be thoroughly cleaned before it appeared, gleaming in the sunshine on race day. Keeping the wire wheels so clean would have been quite a task in itself. Of course, many other owner/drivers looked after their cars in similar fashion, but Gerard and his team seemed to put that little extra effort into making his cars look in the "showroom" condition.

The famous ex Whitney Straight, ex B. Bira 2.9 litre 1934 Maserati owned by H.C. Spero and driven in the Chichester Cup by Cliff Davis.

John Young in the pits (facing camera) with Tony Rolt in the streamlined Connaught and Woodcote corner in the background.

Duncan Hamilton's famous D-Type Jaguar, OKV 1. He finished third in the sports car race for over 2 litre non-supercharged cars behind Roy Salvadori in the Gilby Engineering's DB3S and Mike Sparken in his Ferrari 750 Monza.

Slumbering Ferraris in their overnight accommodation at Wilmott's Garage in Bognor Regis.

My sister, Diana, beside the sort of car that she hoped she might own one day. Rob Walker's 300SL Mercedes.

Goodwood Easter Meeting, 11th April 1955

There was some added excitement in Event 2 at this meeting. This was the five-lap Sports Car Race "A" for cars up to 1500 cc non-supercharged. The lead was a close contest between Les Leston, driving Peter Bell's Connaught AL/SR and Ken McAlpine in the works streamlined Connaught. Leston managed to get in front, just, but on one lap nearly overcooked it at Woodcote, entered the chicane on the wrong line and struck the fencing on the way out, collecting some of the woodwork as he did so. He drove a complete lap with this piece of timber protruding from the offside of his car and managed to deposit it in almost the same spot from whence he took it. He carried on to win the race with McAlpine second and Ivor Bueb in a works Cooper-Climax T39 in third place.

Easter 1955 Rob Walker in his Mercedes 300SL. In the background is Mike Keen's Cooper-Bristol T20.

Easter 1955 Always plenty to look at in the paddock. No. 23 is Horace Richard's 1954 cc HAR in which he finished tenth in the Lavant Cup. No. 61 is R.M. Smith's MG Special. These cars are typical of those regularly seen at Goodwood in Handicap events and at BARC members' meetings.

The new 1072 cc Beart-Rodger-Climax

A very attractive little car which was driven by Stirling Moss in the up to 1500 cc sports car race but which sadly retired with mechanical failure.

The new rear-engined 1098 cc Cooper-Climax

Ivor Bueb drove this car into third place in the up to 1500 cc sports car race.

Two variations of the 2-litre Lister-Bristol

Sandwiched between Brian Lister's Ford Zephyr and a Morris Six is the car which Archie Scott-Brown drove brilliantly to win the up to 2000 cc sports car race. With this same car a few weeks earlier he had won the British Empire Trophy at Oulton Park

And W.B. Black's car which was driven by Jack Sears in the same race at Goodwood.

The shapely Jaguars were seen in action at every Goodwood meeting. From the beautiful XK120 to the very successful D-Type shown above.

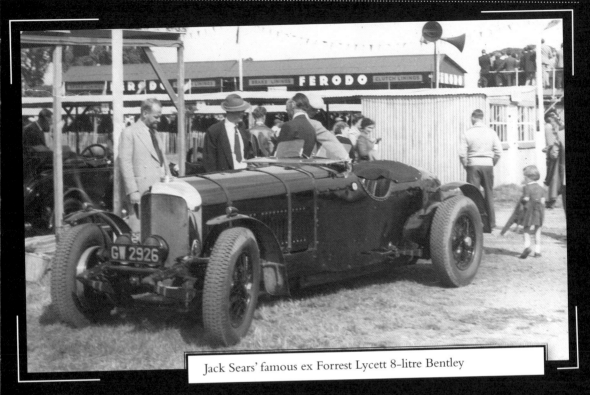

Chapter 8

Jack Sears' famous ex Forrest Lycett 8-litre Bentley

They don't make 'em like that any more!

A meeting of a very different nature took place on 10th September 1955.

The Vintage Sports Car Club held a 21st Birthday Rally. Really it was just a gathering of club members and some of their beautiful cars.

I don't remember how many were there, but there seemed to be hundreds. My notes say that there were 27 Bentleys including Jack Sear's wonderful ex Forrest Lycett 8-litre, two-seater Brooklands car. The tally of Alvis cars was probably just as high and there was a goodly selection of Rolls Royces with a vast selection of different body styles.

Well known VSCC member, Peter Hampton had no less than seven of his cars there that day. Five of these were Bugattis, including the famous "Black Bess" dating from 1913. Also,

The Vintage Sports Car Club's
21st Birthday Rally
10th September 1955

"Black Bess" Peter Hampton's 5027 cc 1913 Bugatti.

H. F. M. Scott's 1924 8-litre Hispano-Suiza.

D. B. Jocelyn's 1925 1081 cc Amilcar.

Cecil Clutton's 1908 12-litre Itala, driven on the day by J.A. Williamson.

A nice line up of Bentleys—27 in all.

S.E. Sears 1914 4-litre GP Opel.

Lord Brabazon sitting in the 100 hp Austin which he drove in the 1908 French Grand Prix.

J.S. Bennett in his well known 1903 Cadillac, which he once drove from Land's End to John o' Groats.

Capt. W.B. Axford RN's 1921 7-litre Napier and R.E. Winn's 1919 3-litre Chevrolet.

1926 Model T Ford Walls Ice Cream van.

L.H. Pagett's
1911 1125 cc Austin.

R. Cann's 1929 7-litre
Mercedes.

he had there a 1903 Mercedes with 9236 cc engine and an 8-litre 1928 Hispano-Suiza. One wonders what his fuel bill was just for attending that one event.

While on the subject of monsters, there were so many that we lost count and they made a real contrast to the many Austin 7s (in various forms) and the Amilcars, Rileys, MGs, Frazer Nash, etc. The Vauxhall contingent, of course, included a few examples of the marvellous 30/98. They were seen in company with some Humbers and Sunbeams and not far away was a Lancia and an OM. Morris, Ford, and Singer were all there, as were Daimler, Alfa Romeo, FIAT, and AC.

There was a good collection of the rare and unusual makes including Star, Bean, Hampton, and GN. The list seemed endless and the day was just not long enough to look at all of them.

All the vehicles were parked in the paddock and beyond, and what a sight it was. Lord

Brabazon was seen sitting in a two-seater Austin, which he had raced in 1908 and F.S. Bennett had brought along his well-known 1903 Cadillac.

Of course, these and a few others are not technically Vintage cars. Many of the cars there that day, were either Veterans or Edwardians but at a wonderful event like this WHO CARES?

J. A. Williamson was driving Cecil Clutton's 1908 12-litre GP Itala and S.E. Sears was driving a 1914 4490 cc GP Opel. The variety seemed to be endless, from 8-litre Hispano-Suiza and 7-litre Napier down to a splendid Model T Ford Walls Ice Cream van.

During the afternoon all these wonderful machines took to the track in a marvellous cavalcade, which proceeded round the circuit in fine style. They were three abreast, as far as the eye could see. It had been a fantastic day and quite unique. G

"I thought the lad could have a go at loading today"

BARC Members Meeting
24th September 1955

I. M. Gillett about to take the chicane in his 3.4 Jaguar to win the five-lap Handicap for saloon cars.

E.P. Heath's XK140.

Beautiful Bugatti!
Believed to be R.C. Symondson's Type 57.

Ten-lap Scratch Race

for sports cars over 1500 cc
and up to 3500 cc.
Photos by Trevor Redman.

Race winner: George Abecassis in his
HWM shared the fastest lap with car
no. 50 at 83.72 mph.

Second: M.W. Head driving Duncan
Hamilton's D-Type Jaguar.

Third: P. Scott-Russell (Lotus-Bristol)
shared the fastest lap with the winner.

Fourth: E. Protheroe (C-Type Jaguar).

74

Chapter 9

Roy Salvadori in his Connaught days.

1956

The Easter meeting of 1956 was run to the usual format and on the whole, was as enjoyable as ever. But it was marred by an accident in the early stages of the Lavant Cup in which Bert Rogers, a well-known Goodwood driver, sadly lost his life when he crashed his Sun-Pat Special. Motor Racing is a dangerous sport and over the years Goodwood has had its share of fatalities. Fortunately not too many, but still upsetting when it happens.

The race was won by Roy Salvadori driving a works Cooper-Climax. Bob Gerard came second in his Cooper-Bristol and third was John Young driving his Connaught.

This race saw Ken Tyrell driving John Coombs' Cooper-Alta as well as his own Cooper-Norton in Event 2, The Earl of March Trophy.

In the Glover Trophy race, Stirling Moss and Roy Salvadori finished first and second in 250F Maseratis. Moss drove a works entry, while Salvadori was driving the Gilby Engineering car. Les Leston and Bob Gerard finished third and fourth, both driving works Connaughts and fifth place was taken by Reg Parnell in a third Connaught entered by Rob Walker.

This race was a good chance to study the differing styles adopted by drivers when driving similar cars. Moss looked as if he was on a relaxed Sunday afternoon drive, while Salvadori was a picture of racing determination. Also, seen on the track at this meeting were Robert Manzon driving the latest Gordini with eight-cylinder engine in the Glover Trophy race, and John Coombs driving his Mercedes 300SL in the production sports car race.

The first race at the Whitsun Meeting, the 26-lap sports car race for cars up to 1500 cc, saw Colin Chapman win in one of his own cars, the Lotus-Climax, and Mike Hawthorn second in a similar car entered by Ecurie Demi-Litre. Third was Jack Brabham driving a works Cooper-Climax. I believe I am right in saying that of the 20 cars, which started this race, 17 were fitted with Climax engines. Quite a record!

As in the previous year, there was a race for vintage cars. This had me jumping up and down. Not such a big field though, but the racing was great to watch. The winner was B.R. Eastick in a 4.6-litre 1930 Bentley. Second was Sir Francis Samuelson in his famous 1914 Sunbeam and third, J.C. Tozer in the little 1927 Amilcar.

All but one of the 22 cars entered in the Madgwick Cup race at the September meeting in 1956 were powered by Climax 1098 cc engines. It seemed that Climax was the unit to have at that time for this class of racing.

However, in the 500 cc race that day, of the 22 cars in the programme at least 17 had Norton power units. A change from just a few years earlier when JAP engines had been favourite.

Roy Salvadori had another good day at the office, he won the Woodcote Cup in a works Cooper-Climax, with Colin Chapman and Les Leston close behind in a Lotus and another Cooper. He won the Sussex Trophy in the same car with the same two second, and third and he finished second to Tony Brooks in the Goodwood Trophy, both driving DB3S Aston Martins. Third in this race was Ron Flockhart in a D-Type Jaguar.

Looking back through the BARC programmes for 1956, for those interested in statistics, I see that in Event 2 at the Easter meeting, the Earl of March Trophy, seven-lap race for 500 cc racing cars, of the 19 which took part, 17 of the cars were powered by Norton engines.

In Event 4 at the same meeting, the seven-lap race for non-supercharged sports cars not exceeding 1500 cc, there were 15 Climax engined cars in a field of 20. The Whit Monday meeting on 21st May saw the same ratio of 15 Climax engines out of 20 in the 26-lap race for these same size sports cars.

The 12-lap race for 500 cc cars that day witnessed another example of Norton power with nine in a field of 14, but at the September meeting that year almost all the cars in the race for 500 cc machines had Norton engines.

In 1956 Cooper cars dominated the 500 cc scene with their various engines, but in those races for the smaller sports car Lotus had a slight edge. In the class for the larger sports cars, there was usually a greater number of Jaguars entered in an event than Aston Martins, but the Astons managed to win their fair share of the prizes.

Easter Meeting
2nd April 1956

All my photographs in this book were taken with two fairly basic cameras. In the early days, a Kodak Brownie Reflex and, from Easter 1955, a 120 GB Kershaw.

Oh, for a zoom lens!

Event 1.
The Lavant Cup

Seven-lap race for non-supercharged cars not exceeding 2000 cc.

Top: Race winner, Roy Salvadori in the works Cooper–Climax, closely followed by second man Bob Gerard in his Cooper–Bristol. Leading from start to finish, the winner's average speed was 87.17 mph. The fastest lap was set by Bob Gerard at 88.89 mph.

Bottom: John Young drove his Connaught into third.

It was on lap one of this race that Bert Rogers crashed his Sun-Pat Special on Lavant corner and sadly was killed.

Event 2.

The Earl of March Trophy

Seven-lap race for 500 cc racing cars.

Top: Ivor Bueb in his race-winning Ecurie Demi-Litre entered Cooper-Norton. Average speed: 83.24 mph. Fastest lap: 84.37 mph.

Middle: C.C.H. Davis driving Francis Beart's Beart-Cooper who finished second, followed by A.V. Cowley's Petty-Norton and others.

Bottom: A.V. Cowley's Petty-Norton being pressed hard by Reg Bicknell in his Revis-Norton and Ken Tyrell in a Cooper-Norton.

Event 3.

Sports Car Race "A"

15-lap scratch race for non-supercharged cars exceeding 1500 cc.

Top: Race winner Stirling Moss in the Gilby Engineering Co. Aston Martin DB3S led from start to finish at an average speed of 89.18 mph and put in the fastest lap at 90.95 mph.

Second down: George Abecassis drove his HWM into second place in his usual calm but impressive manner.

Third down: Bob Berry drove J.C. Broadhead's D-Type Jaguar into third place.

Bottom: M.W. Head and his Cooper-Jaguar finished in sixth place.

Event 4.

Sports Car Race "B"

Seven-lap scratch race for non-supercharged cars up to 1500 cc.

Top: Race winner Roy Salvadori (works Cooper-Climax).

Middle: Reg Bicknell finished fourth in a works Lotus-Climax. Second was Jim Russell in a works Cooper-Climax. Third was Les Leston in the Willment Cooper-Climax.

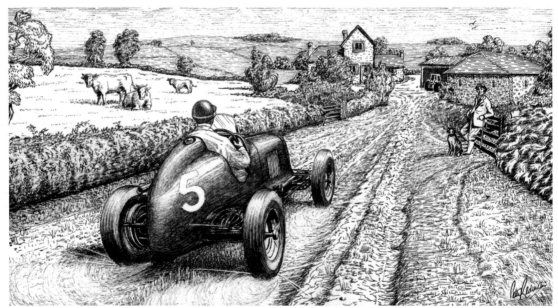

"I must have taken a wrong turning out of the paddock"

Goodwood *Easter 1956*

Photo: Alan R. Smith

Waiting for the flag to drop. Seconds before the start of the Richmond Formula 1 race for the Glover Trophy, over 32 laps. Nearest the camera, Bob Gerard (Connaught), Car no. 4, Mike Hawthorn (BRM Type 25), Car no. 6, Archie Scott-Brown (Connaught), furthest from camera, Stirling Moss (Maserati 250F).

Race result:

1 Stirling Moss (works Maserati 250F)

2 Roy Salvadori (Gilby Engineering Maserati 250F)

3 Les Leston (works Connaught)

4 Bob Gerard (works Connaught)

During this race, when going very well, Mike Hawthorn's car suffered a mechanical failure on Madgwick corner and crashed into the in-field, going end over end and throwing its driver out in the process before landing upside down. Mike Hawthorn suffered only bruising whereas the BRM was rather bent.

Event 5.

The Richmond Trophy

32-lap Formula 1 race.

Top: Race winner Stirling Moss in his works Maserati 250F. He set the fastest lap and new Formula 1 record at 95.79 mph.

Second down: Moss about to lap Archie Scott-Brown's works Connaught.

Third down: Bob Gerard finished fourth in his works Connaught.

Bottom: Mike Hawthorn going well in the BRM before it let him down badly just in front of us on Madgwick corner.

Event 6.

13-lap Production Car Race

Top: Race winner: Ken Rudd (AC-Bristol). His average speed was 78.84 mph and he put in the fastest lap at 80.15 mph.

Second down: Dick Utley drove his Frazer Nash LMR into second place.

John Dalton finished third in his Austin Healey 100S (not shown here, but shown in the paddock on page 91).

Third down: D.J. Calvert finished fourth in his HRG and won Class "C"; seen passing the famous Goodwood haystacks.

Bottom: John Coombs and his shapely Mercedes 300SL.

83

1956 was largely a "sports car and 500" year at Goodwood but very enjoyable none the less. Much of the enjoyment for the spectator was provided by the "other" cars, which made up the field. Events were largely dominated by two or three makes of car, but in the 1950s there would always be a good collection of lesser makes and even the unusual. As mentioned before, Coopers were always there in large numbers in the 500 cc class but Kieft, Revis, Staride, and Beart-Cooper were regulars in the field and often featured in the results. Also, there were such names as Flather-Norton, Jason-Triumph, GM-JAP, Hill Special, Iota, and Petty-Norton to name but a few. The variety of makes in this class and the number of vehicles in each race made a real spectacle for the spectator and I believe helped to make Goodwood what it is.

In events for the smaller sports car, it was great to see in the programme, and then on the track, such names as Frazer Nash, MG, Elva, Tojeiro, Halselec, and Fairthorpe among the Cooper and Lotus brigade.

When it came to the races for the larger sports car, Jaguar, Aston Martin, and Ferrari were always there but mixing it with them would be a strong contingent from Connaught, HWM, Lister, Cooper, and Tojeiro. Variety in the Sussex countryside was what made it always such a good day out. ᵷ

Event 7. Seven-lap Easter Handicap
Left: race winner Ron Flockhart in the Ecurie Ecosse D-Type Jaguar.
Right: Bob Gerard (Cooper-Bristol).

Whit-Monday 1956
Vintage Car Handicap Race, five laps

1st

B.R. Eastick 1930 Bentley 4½ litre.

2nd

Sir Francis Samuelson 1914 Sunbeam 3.3 litre.

6th

R.G.H. Clutton 1927 1098 cc s/c Amilcar. J.C. Tozer, in a matching Amilcar, finished in third place. Both cars were entered by T.N.C. Engineering Co. Tozer was scratch and Clutton had 45 seconds start. Eastick's Bentley had just 3 seconds start and Samuelson's Sunbeam 1 minute 55 seconds.

26-Lap Sports Car Race

Ron Flockhart
Ecurie Ecosse D-Type
Jaguar second to Bob Berry.

*Ron Flockhart
and Desmond
Titterington*
Ecurie Ecosse D-Types.

Archie Scott-Brown
Lister-Maserati.

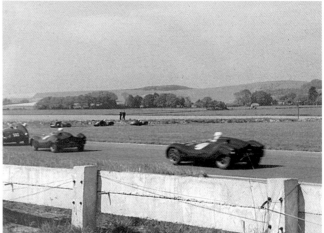

Leaving Madgwick

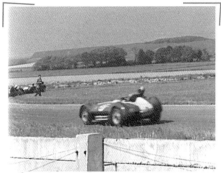

Archie Scott-Brown
Lister-Maserati.

Bob Berry Jaguar D-Type. Winner 26-lap race for Sports Cars non-supercharged exceeding 1500 cc.

Jim Russell Cooper-Norton. Winner 12-lap race for 500 cc.

Colin Chapman Lotus-Climax
Doing his lap of honour after winning the 28-lap Sports Car Race "A" for non-supercharged up to 1500 cc.

87

September 1956
500 cc Race

First Jim Russell (Cooper)

Jim in his new Cooper in the paddock and in the pit lane.

Ivor Bueb (Cooper)

who finished fifth in the race.

Jim Russell recording the work being done on his works Cooper–Norton and then discussing progress with Ivor Bueb (in cap) and another driver (below).

Jim Russell won the five-lap 500 cc race. Don Parker was second and Stuart Lewis-Evans third, all driving Cooper-Nortons.

Works Tojeiro-Climax driven by G. Rolls.

Equipe Devone Aston Martin DB3S driven by T. Kyffin.

8th September 1956
The Goodwood Trophy

21-lap race for non-supercharged sports cars exceeding 1500 cc.

Works Aston Martin DB3S cars of Roy Salvadori (no. 5) and Tony Brooks (no. 6), plus the private entry DB3S (no. 8) of Graham Whitehead. Tony Brooks won the Goodwood Trophy race and Roy Salvadori finished second. Ron Flockhart was third in the Ecurie Ecosse D-Type Jaguar.

Roy Salvadori takes the works Aston Martin DB3S down the Start and Finish straight.

The Ecurie Ecosse team of D-Type Jaguars entered in the 21-lap Goodwood Trophy. No. 1, Ron Flockhart (finished second), no. 2, Ninian Sanderson (fifth) and no. 3, J. Lawrence (sixth). In the background, the Cooper-Climax of P.D. Gammon who finished fifth in the Madgwick Cup.

C.P. McNaughton's 1100 cc Elva-Ford.

Ivor Bueb out for a stroll.

Ron Flockhart
D-Type Jaguar of
Ecurie Ecosse.

E. Protheroe,
who finished seventh
entering the pit lane in
the works HWM, while
Ninian Sanderson steams
past in the second Ecurie
Ecosse D-Type.

The beautiful lines of the Lotus Eleven Climax entered and driven by G.M. Jones.
Car no. 89 is G.B. Hewitt's earlier model.

Chapter 10

J.F. Dalton's Austin Healey 100S—Easter 1955.

An interesting change

A slight departure from the "norm" heralded the Easter meeting of 1957. *Autosport* magazine ran a series of races at different circuits throughout the year for production sports cars and the meeting's first race that day carried with it some points towards this Championship. It was a 13-lap scratch race divided into three classes. It was great to see nearly 30 cars, just like those we would see on a daily basis on our local roads, dicing with one another at break-neck speeds around the track. And in the space of 13 laps there were quite a few incidents of excursions on to the grass, gyrating cars on corners, bodyworks exchanging paint, and a few shaking fists.

The list of cars entered was both interesting and varied, and the results reflect this. Outright winner was Ken Rudd driving an AC Ace. He also won the class for 1501–2700 cc. Second was Dickie Stoop in a Frazer Nash. Third was J. Dalton in an Austin Healey 100S and, fourth, R.J.W. Utley in another Frazer Nash.

The other class winners were: up to 1500 cc, T. Barnard driving a Lotus-Ford; and over 2700 cc, P.J. Sargent in a Jaguar XK120.

The rest of the day followed the usual pattern and was just as exciting as ever. The Lavant Cup (12 laps to Formula 2) was once again full of Climax-engined Cooper and Lotus cars. Tony Brooks kept the Rob Walker Cooper ahead of Jack Brabham in the works car and third was Ron Flockhart in John Coombs' Lotus.

The Chichester Cup (10-lap sports car race up to 1500 cc) was a clean sweep for Lotus. Colin Chapman driving his works car was followed by Ron Flockhart driving John Coombs' car and Keith Hall in a second works car.

The Formula 1 race for the Glover Trophy was fast and furious. A battle between Vanwall, BRM, Connaught, and Cooper developed which was, eventually, won by the B-Type Connaught: Archie Scott-Brown in a works car ahead of Jack Fairman driving Rob Walker's. Third place went to Ron Flockhart in the BRM Type 25. Then followed Jack Brabham in a works Cooper-Climax, Jim Russell driving the Gilby 250F Maserati, and Tony Brooks in a Vanwall. Though he only managed sixth place, Tony Brooks had the satisfaction of setting a new lap record at 96.43 mph.

The 21-lap Sussex Trophy race for the larger sports cars produced quite a scrap between a variety of cars. There were five D-Type Jaguars, four Aston Martins, two Cooper-Jaguars, two HWM-Jaguars, a Lotus-Bristol, a couple of Listers, one with a Jag engine and the other with Maserati power, and a few other cars for good measure. Mid field during the race there was a good deal of place swapping and up front the pace was really fast and furious. Try as they did, Roy Salvadori in the DBR1 and Tony Brooks in the DB3S (both works cars) just could not catch the flying Archie Scott-Brown in the works Lister-Jaguar. He appeared to be taking the corners without lifting his right foot at all. How he kept his car on the black stuff we shall never know.

Lap after lap he kept coming through Madgwick, on the same line and at the same pace. It was breathtaking. We felt sure that any minute he would over-cook it and take to the grass. But no, he was so accurate and so fast it was like watching an automaton. Very exciting, but not so good for the blood pressure.

Eventually he took the chequered flag and a tremendous cheer went up from right around the circuit. They must have heard it in Chichester. Salvadori and Brooks came in second and third, followed by Duncan Hamilton (D-Type Jaguar), Peter Blond (HWM-Jaguar), and Graham Whitehead (DB3S). As well as winning the race, Archie Scott-Brown had set up a new sports car lap record of 91.33 mph. It is interesting to see in the programme a certain G. Hill as driver of C. T. Atkins' DB3S. Was this his first drive on this circuit?

The day was rounded off by the ten-lap 500 cc race for the Earl of March Trophy. There were more JAP engines in this race but they were still out-numbered by the Nortons, which executed a clean sweep at the finish. Stuart Lewis-Evans had his second win of the day, this time driving Francis Beart's Beart-Cooper-Norton. E. Hall came second and D. Strange, third, both driving Cooper-Nortons.

So the year was off to a very good start with a most exciting meeting. Once again all the spectators went home with smiles on their faces. And there was no "aggro" in the queues to get out of the car parks.

The Whitsun meeting had a few surprises in store for the spectators, which were all most enjoyable. The first event was a seven-lap handicap for closed cars. It was won by John Sprinzel driving an Austin A35. Second was J.K. Bell in a Morris Minor and third, W.G. Wright in a Morris 1000. Jean Bloxham recorded the fastest lap at 76.60 mph in her Aston Martin DB2, while trying desperately to carve her way through a field of mostly quite ordinary looking cars.

There were two sports car races with the usual selection of Aston Martins, Jaguars, Coopers, and Lotuses, but the two most exciting events of the day were one for Bentleys and a Ladies Handicap.

The race of the day was a seven-lap handicap for pre-war Bentleys. The sight and sound of these very substantial machines roaring round the track was wonderful. Towards the end of

the race, when they began to bunch up, it was almost unbelievable. They were even going through the chicane two abreast.

The event was won by Donald Day in a fairly standard 1925 3-litre model (he had a good handicap credit), but was hotly pursued by M.J. Bradley and A.P.K. Chaffrey.

The fastest lap was recorded by George Burton in a much modified 3-litre, which had a four-and-a-half litre engine with three carburettors squeezed in, plus de-Dion rear axle and hydraulic brakes. Because of these modifications it was, of course, heavily handicapped, but in spite of this he finished fourth, having put in a lap at 77.00 mph. How he managed to overtake all those other rather cumbersome machines on this narrow track in just seven laps without coming to grief remains a mystery. The winner's average speed was a creditable 65.11 mph.

Contrast in power
After a practice session, the Ecurie Ecosse team of 3442 cc D-Type Jaguars wait behind a 500 cc Cooper.

The Ladies Handicap was run over five laps and with an interesting collection of cars entered. Some ladies were obviously far more at home on a race track than others, but they all put up a good show. This event was won by Avril Scott-Moncrieff in nifty style, driving a little Lotus-MG MkVI. Second was Rosemary Seers in a Cooper-Zephyr T14 and third was Jean Bloxham. Once again showing how to storm through the field in a DB2. And again she recorded the fastest lap of the race at 77.14 mph.

There was a lady winner of the sports car Handicap at the September meeting of 1957. Patsy Burt won in fine style in her 1098 cc Cooper-Climax. She had a 50 second start over scratch man Duncan Hamilton in his D-Type Jaguar, but drove with great determination to keep her car in front of several matching Coopers, some Lotus-Climaxes, an XK120, two more D-Types, some DB3Ss, and an assortment of other machinery.

In the Goodwood Trophy race, Archie Scott-Brown again proved that he was unbeatable in the works Lister-Jaguar. Jack Brabham finished second driving a Tojeiro-Jaguar, ahead of Henry Taylor in a D-Type Jaguar, with Roy Salvadori fourth driving John Coombs' Lotus-Climax.

Salvadori had previously won the Formula 2 Woodcote Cup from Jack Brabham, both driving works Cooper-Climaxes. Brabham having put in the fastest lap at 96.00 mph.

"West Indies are all out for 182!"

Ken Wharton

Although very successful elsewhere with his
ERA R11B in hill-climbs, etc., Goodwood
spectators will remember him well for his
spirited drives in his Frazer Nash LMR, with
which he gained a second place and two thirds,
but more especially for his handling of the V16
BRM. With these fantastic machines, at the
September meeting of 1952 he finished third
in the Goodwood Trophy, at the Easter 1953
meeting he finished second in the Chichester
Cup, and then went on to win the Glover
Trophy. At the September meeting that year, he
finished second in the Goodwood Trophy and
third in the Woodcote Cup.

In 1954, at the Easter meeting, he won the
Glover Trophy with the V16 and then won
the Chichester Cup with the P30 Mk II. At
the September meeting he took the P30 for
another outing and finished second in the
Woodcote Cup.

27th September 1952, five-lap sports car race
Ken Wharton (Frazer Nash LMR), third at St Mary's.
Tony Rolt (Jaguar C-Type), winner, Stirling Moss (Jaguar C-Type), second.

The Madgwick Cup race was a clean sweep for Lotus. Team Lotus claimed first, second, and third, the drivers being Stacey, Hall, and Ashdown, while Ivor Bueb drove the similar "Demi-Litre" car into fourth place.

With the usual 500 cc and another sports car race filling the afternoon, the Goodwood year was drawing to a close. And what fun it had been. I'm sure that the drivers had enjoyed it too, or most of them. But once again we, the spectators, were indebted to all the drivers, mechanics, marshals, and the many, many other people involved in providing such wonderful entertainment for us throughout the season. We all went home safe in the knowledge that they will be back next year to do it all over again.

Although Madgwick was our favourite area from which to watch the racing, we did try some other places from time to time. One of the great assets of Goodwood, after the first few meetings had convinced the organisers that they were on to a good thing, was the fact that spectators could move freely from one vantage point to another; from one enclosure to another. Every part of the course is visible. During a meeting, each race could be watched from a different position. Over the years we tried most of them.

Lavant Corner can be exciting from the enclosure at the beginning of the Lavant Straight, with the cars coming towards you at many different angles. Woodcote, if viewed from that end of the Lavant Straight, is quite different as you watch the cars from behind as they take the corner and head for the chicane. There can be some hairy moments just here. It can be very exciting to watch from near the Chicane, but

it is not possible to see much of the rest of the circuit from here.

From the start of St Mary's and looking back down Fordwater, the cars are coming straight at you and then turn right into St Mary's. Try watching from here through binoculars. You will scare yourself to death.

Different parts of Madgwick all have good points. The northern end is great for watching the starts and finishes of races, and the cars can be watched from behind as they all fight to get round the corner. Sometimes there are those who don't make it. Towards the western end of the enclosure is also fun, as you can watch their progress from just after the start, right round the corner and through Fordwater until they disappear through St Mary's. I don't believe that there is such a thing as a bad position for spectators at Goodwood.

A great aspect of motor racing in the 50s, and very evident at Goodwood, was that the likes of John Cooper, Colin Chapman, and Jack Brabham and, of course, a few other lesser mortals, raced cars which they had built themselves. However, the three named above are the best known, not only because they achieved great and international success with their cars, but also because they were all very successful drivers. They continued in the spirit set all those years ago at Brooklands. I well remember reading reports in the papers and magazines at the time saying: "John Cooper wins in a Cooper", "Colin Chapman wins in his Lotus" and "Jack Brabham and his Brabham beat all the opposition".

Those days are long gone, but fortunately many examples of their cars are still very active in Historic Races such as those held at Goodwood. Spectators can still enjoy the sights and sounds of all of them thanks to the efforts and dedication (and money) lavished on them by their present owners. With the aid of modern technology, the engines and tyres are now so good that most of these cars are now lapping at speeds unthinkable when they were new. Their drivers must frighten themselves silly at times. ℭ

Jack Brabham in the works Cooper-Climax finished second to Stirling Moss in Rob Walker's similar car in the 1959 Easter Monday Goodwood International "100" for the Glover Trophy.

Rear engines get in front

By the late 1950s, Lotus cars were beginning to dominate the 1100cc sports car class. They had managed to elbow the Coopers a bit to one side and thought that they had a clear road ahead. However, they did not have things all their own way when the Lola-Climax began to establish itself as a serious rival and started to win races.

At about this time the Cooper-Climax was the car to beat in Formula 2 and the Formula 1 version was fast becoming a serious championship contender. In 1959 Jack Brabham won the Driver's title for himself and the Constructor's title for Cooper. It is said that the great Enzo Ferrari dismissed the rear-engined cars as a flash in the pan. But really the writing was clearly on the wall.

The line up of cars at the 1958 Easter meeting at Goodwood is interesting. The 15-lap Lavant Cup for Formula 2 cars produced a field of nine

Coopers and three Lotus cars and the ten-lap Chichester Cup race for Sports Cars up to 1100cc had 20 Lotus, three Elva, and one Tojeiro.

The main event of the day, the Glover Trophy race, had a good selection of Lotus and Cooper cars among the more traditional Maseratis, BRMs, Connaughts, and Ferrari. Mike Hawthorn won in his Ferrari, but Coopers were second and third (Brabham and Salvadori), and a Lotus was fourth.

There were plenty of interesting drivers and cars in the programme.

The first event of the day, the 500cc Earl of March Trophy race saw Beart-Cooper-Nortons (Cooper-Nortons breathed on by Francis Beart) finish first and second driven by Stuart Lewis-Evans and Trevor Taylor.

Jack Brabham won the 15-lap Formula 2 Lavant Cup driving a Cooper-Climax and Graham Hill was second in a Lotus–Climax. Cooper and Lotus were becoming almost unbeatable.

The 21-lap Sussex Trophy race for the big sports cars was, as usual, fast and furious. Stirling Moss took the chequered flag at the finish in the new Aston Martin DBR2, setting a new lap record in the process at 92.50 mph. Peter Collins drove a Ferrari Dino 206s into second place and Duncan Hamilton was third in his D–Type Jaguar.

As mentioned earlier, the Formula 1 race for the Glover Trophy had a mixture of front and rear engined cars. At 42-laps on this small circuit it is a strain on both car and driver. It can be quite taxing for the spectators in the enclosures too. Feet and legs take a pounding. It is not much good sitting down (unless you are lucky enough to be in a really good position), as you are bound to miss the most exciting incident of the day.

As usual there were mechanical retirements and off the road excursions which sometimes meant a retirement also. By the end of the race the field was considerably reduced in size and spread over several laps. For the spectator it was sometimes difficult to remember who was on which lap. If too much time was spent filling in the lap chart (very kindly supplied by the organisers in the programme), once again it was possible that something might happen on the track while your head was down.

I believe that this was the only time a works Ferrari won a race at Goodwood. Cliff Allison was fourth behind Brabham and Salvadori, and in fifth and sixth places were Connaught Bs driven by Stuart Lewis-Evans and Archie Scott-Brown. These two had been entered by someone by the name of Bernie Ecclestone.

Stirling Moss driving Rob Walker's Cooper–Climax and Mike Hawthorn in the Ferrari

both put in laps of 97.30 mph to set a new record.

It was sports cars all the way for the Whitsun meeting of 1958 except for a marvellous Historic Cars race over 10 laps. Once again we were able to watch these wonderful old machines thundering round the circuit, sliding round the corners, their drivers fighting with the steering wheels. Side by side down the straight, no quarter given and into Woodcote together. Wheels onto the grass and still nothing between them. Finally, one has to yield as they squeeze through the chicane. The one behind is sideways, wheels in all directions. How does he stay on the track? Now he is straight again and blasts his way past the pits, chasing hard all the way to Madgwick where the battle begins all over again.

It was a real ERA race. Won by Bill Moss driving ERA R5B with Douglas Hull second, driving ERA R11B. Third was J. Goodhew driving the famous ERA-Delage. A really great race, which rather overshadowed the rest of the meeting as far as I was concerned.

The day had started with an *Autosport* production sports car race over 12 laps. As I have said before, it was great to see all these normal "road" cars dicing with one another and being given the chance to show just how fast they can go. AC-Bristols finished first and third, driven by Ted Whiteaway and Mike Anthony, making a Frazer Nash sandwich of Bill Wilks. Whiteaway put in a very respectable fastest lap at 80.15 mph.

Duncan Hamilton and Graham Whitehead had a fight over who should have the Whitsun Trophy. Whitehead eventually bringing his Lister-Jaguar home in front of the D-Type. However, Duncan Hamilton got his 3.4 Jaguar to the flag first in the Production Saloon

Car race ahead of Tommy Sopwith and Sir Gawaine Baillie driving similar cars.

There were two more ten-lap sports car races that day. Jack Sears drove his Austin Healey 100/6 into first place in the "Marque" race ahead of Paul Fletcher's AC Ace. And in the Whitsun Handicap, Bruce Halford chalked up another win for Lister-Jaguar ahead of Bob Hicks' Lotus-Climax 11 and Duncan Hamilton in the D-Type after his usual spirited drive, carving his way through the field from the back. G

More from the paddock

Mike Sparken's 3 litre Ferrari.

C. Wick's ex-Whitehead Cooper-Maserati.

The new Sunbeam Talbot 90.

The Goodwood International "100" for the Glover Trophy

Easter 1958

42-lap scratch race for Grand Prix cars

The cars scream away from the start towards Madgwick corner, Jean Behra in the BRM in the lead. Note how close to the track the photographer is standing.

Mike Hawthorn driving the works Ferrari on his way to victory. Together with Stirling Moss, they set the fastest lap at 97.30 mph.

Roy Salvadori and Jack Brabham driving their works Coopers ahead of Graham Hill's works Lotus. Brabham finished second and Salvadori was third.

Archie Scott-Brown
in Bernie Ecclestone's Connaught.

Stuart Lewis-Evans
in Bernie Ecclestone's other
Connaught, the "Dart", also known as
the "Toothpaste tube".

Jean Behra in the works BRM.

Stirling Moss about to lap a back marker.

In the Formula 2 race, a Cooper had a bit of a confrontation with the straw bales. Perhaps it did not have "Mintex" brakes! The marshals and photographers were quickly on the scene but wisely did not stray onto the track.

The Lavant Cup
15-lap race for Formula 2 Cars

Graham Hill in the Team Lotus Lotus-Climax, who finished in second place, about to be passed by race winner Jack Brabham in the works Cooper-Climax.

Cliff Allison in the Team Lotus Lotus-Climax finished third.

Stuart Lewis-Evans driving the BRP-entered Cooper-Climax finished fourth.

Stirling Moss drove Rob Walker's Cooper-Climax in both the Lavant Cup and the Glover Trophy. He did not feature in the results, but together with Mike Hawthorn set the fastest lap in the Glover Trophy at 97.30 mph.

The Sussex Trophy
21-lap scratch race for non-s/c sports cars exceeding 1100 cc, with a Le Mans type start

When the flag fell, Moss made his customary high-speed sprint across the track to leap into his car and had a substantial lead by the time he reached Madgwick corner for the first time.

Peter Collins in the works Ferrari on his way to take second place behind Moss.

Duncan Hamilton in his privately entered D-Type finished third.

Bruce Halford in his Lister-Jaguar about to be lapped by race winner, Stirling Moss in the works Aston Martin DBR2. Moss' winning average speed was 89.94 mph and he set a new sports car lap record at 92.50 mph.

Graham Whitehead drove his privately entered Aston Martin DB3S into fourth place.

Stirling Moss and Archie Scott-Brown in close company.

Mrs Jean Bloxham driving the Aston Martin DB3S coupe entered by Gerrards Cross Motor Co.

Archie Scott-Brown in the works Lister-Jaguar.

Willie Mairesse driving the Equipe Nationale Belge entered Lister-Jaguar.

C.A.S. "Tony" Brooks

A driver with great talent hidden beneath a very calm exterior. Between Easter 1955 and September 1959 he clocked up wins with both DB3S Aston Martin and Cooper-Climax T41, two second places with the Frazer Nash LMR and third places (twice) with DB3S and with a Ferrari 250TR59 in the 24th RAC Tourist Trophy.

In 1957 he showed us how he could handle a Vanwall, before taking off to do great things with it on the circuits of Europe.

An unspectacular driver to watch but very fast and with great overtaking skills. Spectators were always pleased to find his name in the programme.

Easter Monday 22nd April 1957
Richmond Formula 1 Race for the Glover Trophy.
Tony Brooks in the new Vanwall at Madgwick. He set a new lap record at 96.43 mph, but finished in sixth place due to mechanical trouble. (Race winner: Stuart Lewis-Evans, Connaught "B".)

Chapter 12

Through the chicane! Tony Brooks in the Aston Martin DBR1, which he and Stirling Moss drove to victory in the 23rd RAC Tourist Trophy race on 13th September 1958.

The "TT" cometh

On 13th September 1958 Goodwood was host to the 23rd RAC Tourist Trophy Race. It is difficult to describe an event of this magnitude, which can be full of incidents in just a few words. Most of the top drivers and makes of car assembled to pit their skills and powers of endurance against each other, all ably supported by their dedicated pit crews for a race which lasted for just over four hours.

The Tourist Trophy race had not been held since 1955 and never before on the Goodwood circuit. There was a distinct air of expectation. Once again the Sussex track proved to be lucky for Aston Martin. They finished first, second, and third in close formation after 148 laps, and in the same order in which they had formed up for the Le Mans type start. Stirling Moss and Tony Brooks shared the leading DBR1 with Moss setting a new out and out sports car lap record at 93.30 mph. The second car was driven by Roy Salvadori and Jack

Brabham, and the third by Carroll Shelby and Stuart Lewis-Evans.

Fourth place was taken by Jean Behra and Edgar Bath driving a Porsche RSK, fifth a Jaguar D-Type driven by Masten Gregory and Innes Ireland, and Duncan Hamilton and Peter Blond brought their D-Type home in sixth place.

Understandably, there had been quite a few retirements along the way and, as usual with a long distance race of this nature, the back markers were several laps down at the finish. But a lasting impression of the day is that the Aston Martins seemed to run like clockwork from start to finish. Drivers and pit crews obviously working very well together.

The Easter meeting of 1959 was very much to the usual format with five events: Formula 1, Formula 2, large sports cars, small sports cars, and saloons. However, the number of makes of car which featured in the first three places of all the races that day was remarkably small, only six.

Event 1, the Chichester Cup 10-lap race for sports cars up to 1100 cc, was a Lola-Climax 1-2-3. Peter Ashdown, Peter Gammon, and Michael Taylor being the drivers in a race which had only four Lolas racing against about 10 Lotus-Climax, a handful of Elvas, and one or two others.

Event 2, the Lavant Cup 15-lap race for Formula 2 racing cars, was a 1-2-3 for Cooper-Climax. The drivers in this case being Jack Brabham, Roy Salvadori, and Jim Russell. This race was heavily weighed in favour of the Coopers, although not all had Climax engines.

The Sussex Trophy Race came next. As before, this was a 21-lap event for the larger sports cars and with a Le Mans type start. The usual variety of makes lined up in front of the pits and there was the mad dash across the

track for the drivers when the flag fell. This was always fun to watch and became exciting when some of the faster cars were slower off the mark and then had to fight their way through the pack. Naturally, at the beginning of a race even the slower cars were not going to give way to anybody and for several laps there would be passing and re-passing and the occasional fist shaking. Eventually the race would settle down and two or three private battles would develop sometimes going on throughout the entire race.

Lister-Jaguars finished first and second. Ivor Bueb driving the works car and J. Sieff second in his own car. Graham Whitehead came third in the Aston Martin DBR1.

The main event of the day, The Goodwood International "100" for the Glover Trophy was a contest between front and rear engines: BRM versus Cooper. There were, of course, other cars in the form of Maserati and Lotus, but at the finish the first six places were filled with Cooper and BRM. Stirling Moss, driving Rob Walker's Cooper-Climax won the race at an average speed of 90.31 mph. Jack Brabham driving a works Cooper-Climax finished in second place ahead of Harry Schell in a BRM Type 25. Jo Bonnier was fourth in the other BRM and Masten Gregory and Bruce McLaren brought in the other two works Coopers fifth and sixth.

The last event of the day, The Fordwater Trophy, was a 10-lap race for saloon cars and divided into classes for different size engines. However, the first three cars to cross the line were all Jaguars. Ivor Bueb had his second win of the day driving the Equipe Endeavour 3.4. Roy Salvadori drove John Coombs' similar car into second place and third was Sir Gawaine Baillie in his own machine. Fords did well in the smaller classes, which had a collection

The Gilby Engineering Co.'s 2-litre Sports Maserati with which Roy Salvadori won the five-lap race for non-supercharged Sports Cars up to 2000 cc in September 1954.

of Austins, a pair of Borgwards, and representatives of Riley, Wolseley, Morris, Renault, Hillman, and Peerless.

Once again, races for sports and touring cars predominated at the Whitsun meeting in 1959, but as before there was a race for pre-war racing cars. The first race of the day was a 10-lap event for Touring and Grand Touring cars. It was nice to see the new Lotus Elites in action, and finishing in first and third positions.

Easter Monday 2nd April 1956
Unlimited Sports Car race—Fordwater.
Stirling Moss (Gilby Engineering Aston Martin DB3S), winner.

Peter Lumsden and John Lawry being the drivers. Second spot was filled by Sir Gawaine Baillie in his Jaguar 3.4.

Next up was the best race of the day as far as I was concerned, the 10-lap event for pre-war racing cars. With very much the same line up as the previous year, the air was soon filled with the sounds and smells only associated with these wonderful pieces of machinery hurtling round the circuit, their drivers throwing them into the corners and coming out at almost impossible angles. Wheel to wheel combat was the name of the game. Douglas Hull, who finished second last year, won the race in his ERA R11B. Gordon Chapman made it a 1–2 for ERA by finishing second in R2A and J. Goodhew brought his famous ERA-Delage

into third spot. He had finished second last year.

Jaguar engines were working well in the Whitsun Trophy race and the First Whitsun Handicap. The 21-lap Whitsun Trophy saw a clean sweep by them. Ron Flockhart won driving a Tojeiro, second was John Bekaert, and third, Peter Blond, both driving Listers.

In the First Whitsun Handicap, John Coundley driving a D-Type Jaguar finished second and Peter Blond came third again in the Lister. The winner of this race was Richard Utley driving a Lotus-Climax 11.

The "Marque" sports car race saw a struggle at the front between TR3s and Morgan+4 for most of the 10 laps culminating in a Morgan sandwich at the finish. Syd Hurrell and Bill de Selincourt were the

"Don't worry – it'll be a doddle"

Easter Monday 2nd April 1956
Glover Trophy Race (Formula 1)—St Mary's.
Mike Hawthorn (BRM Type 25). Winner: Stirling Moss (Works Maserati 250F).

drivers of the Triumphs and Chris Lawrence the Morgan.

The Second Whitsun Handicap was great fun, with the cars getting closer and closer together as the race progressed. This 10-lap race being much more fun than the more usual five-lap version. There was the customary assortment of everyday cars which circulated at much greater speed than they should on the highway and the drivers were dicing with one another all round the circuit. Ding-dong battles developed even back to the tail-

enders and at times it was hard to see where the leading cars were. Paul Fletcher drove his MG-A across the line to win from Bill de Selincourt in his Triumph TR3. Third was Chris Lawrence driving his Morgan+4: reverse order for these two from the earlier race.

The 24th RAC Tourist Trophy Race was held on the 5th September 1959. This was the second time that Goodwood played host to this event and certainly a day to remember. Aston Martin won for the second year running but in very different circumstances.

However, in doing so they clinched the World Sports Car Championship.

The day will be remembered for two reasons. First, for the fire which destroyed the leading Aston Martin and the team's pits and second, for the way in which Tony Brooks set about trying to catch the leading cars towards the end of the race. Everything was going well for the Aston Martin team in the early stages of the race and a repeat of last year's 1-2-3 looked a distinct possibility. Stirling Moss had established a substantial lead and handed over to Roy Salvadori who consolidated it.

Some two and a half hours into the race, Salvadori came into the pits at the end of his session to re-fuel and change tyres and to hand the car back to Moss. Some fuel spilt and the heat from the exhaust pipe caused the car to be engulfed in flames. Salvadori was injured, but fortunately not seriously. However, the car and the Aston Martin pits were wrecked. Graham Whitehead, who was driving his own privately entered Aston Martin, immediately withdrew his car so that the works team could use his pit area.

Only minutes after the fire had started, Jack Fairman, who was sharing the second works Aston Martin with Carroll Shelby, brought it in for a routine pit stop. Even though they were in an unfamiliar pit, the crew got the car back onto the track in 57 seconds. However, Moss was now at the wheel instead of Shelby with the car lying in second place, some 30 seconds behind Jo Bonnier's Porsche. Salvadori's injuries prevented him from driving again that day, so Moss drove for the remainder of the race, about four hours and crossed the line to win his fifth Tourist Trophy. And very well deserved.

Ferrari did a bit of driver swapping also, but for different reasons. Tony Brooks was sharing a 250 with Dan Gurney and during the afternoon had set fastest lap of the day at 94.12 mph. This was a new sports car lap record. With about an hour to go in the race, the sister car of Olivier Gendebien and Giulio

24th RAC Tourist Trophy Race, 5th September 1959
Left: Stirling Moss in the ill-fated DBR1 early in the race. Right: Almost there—Stirling Moss takes the winning DBR1 into the chicane on the last lap. Photos: Trevor Redman.

Cabianca was ahead of Tony Brooks' machine, so it was called into the pits so that Brooks could take it over and set about trying to catch the leading cars. He drove like the wind but ran out of time and finished a very creditable third. Phil Hill had a stint in this car also, as his own, which he was sharing with Cliff Allison, expired early in the race with engine trouble.

Bonnier and von Tripps drove a cracking race in the little Porsche, at one time leading the race. They could not match the pace set by Moss, but managed to keep ahead of Brooks in the flying Ferrari and finished a very creditable

second. In the process they broke the Class B sports car lap record several times, von Tripps eventually setting it at 92.90 mph very near the end of the race.

There had been the usual excitement among the other cars with several private battles going on and a few agricultural excursions. A number of mechanical failures meant that the field was a lot smaller at the finish which, for the spectator, makes it easier to work out who is on which lap. The winning car completed 224 laps, whereas even the car which finished in sixth place had done only 210. The final results were:

Result of the 24th RAC Tourist Trophy Race

1 Carroll Shelby/Jack Fairman/Stirling Moss
(Aston Martin DBR1)

2 Wolfgang von Tripps/Jo Bonnier (Porsche RS60)

3 Olivier Gendebien/Giulio Cabianca/Tony Brooks/Phil Hill
(Ferrari 250)

4 Maurice Trentignant/Paul Frere (Aston Martin DBR1)

5 Tony Brooks/Dan Gurney (Ferrari 250)

6 Peter Ashdown/Alan Ross (Lola-Climax)

The team award this time going to Lola. **G**

More from the car park

Healey Silverstone

Austin Somerset

Austin Devon

Austin Atlantic

Rolls Royce

Chapter 13

Easter Monday 22nd April 1957—St Mary's
Goodwood International "100" for the Glover Trophy, 42 laps, Formula 1.
Roy Salvadori (Cooper-Climax), third. Cliff Allison (Lotus-Climax), fourth. Stuart Lewis-Evans (Connaught "B"), fifth. [Race winner: Mike Hawthorn (Ferrari Dino 246).]

The shape of things to come

1960 confirmed the dawning of a new era in motor racing. The front-engined single-seater was already an endangered species and the smaller sports car was heading the same way. The larger engined sports car would hold its own for a while yet, but the writing had been on the wall for some time. Fortunately, the Goodwood crowd had more sense than to write on walls and came to enjoy the racing whatever the shape of the cars. However, the rear-engined brigade was mounting a take-over.

The Easter Meeting was a real Lotus and Cooper day with a Porsche and a couple of BRMs managing to squeeze in on the act.

For saloon cars it was the usual battle between Aston Martin and Jaguar.

The Chichester Cup race was for Formula Junior cars over ten laps and Lotus-Ford 18s filled the first three places. The drivers being: Jim Clark (we would see a lot of him in later years), Trevor Taylor, and Mike McKee.

The Formula 2 Lavant Cup race over 15 laps had variety at the finish with Innes Ireland getting there first in the new works Lotus-Climax 18. Try as they did, Stirling Moss in Rob Walker's Porsche 718 and Roy Salvadori in the Cooper-Climax could not catch him.

Roy Salvadori made up for it in the Sussex Trophy race for sports cars by finishing first in a Cooper-Monaco. Second in this 21-lap race was Jimmy Blumer in another Cooper-Monaco and third, Tom Dickson driving a Lotus-Climax.

Records were being broken in every race. Jim Clark set a new Formula Junior lap at 92.31 mph. Innes Ireland set a new Formula 2 lap at 97.30 mph and Roy Salvadori put in a lap for sports cars at 96.43 mph.

The Goodwood International "100" for the Glover Trophy that day was another fine win for Innes Ireland and the new Lotus-Climax. In this race Stirling Moss drove Rob Walker's Cooper-Climax but could not catch the flying Ireland and had to accept second place. Chris Bristow finished third and Bruce McLaren fourth, both driving Cooper-Climax cars, a T51 and a T45. Graham Hill was fifth in a BRM P48 and Jo Bonnier sixth driving a BRM Type 25.

The last race of the day saw a real ding-dong battle between Stirling Moss and Roy Salvadori. These two often drove for the same team and indeed on many occasions shared the same car, so it was interesting to see them in different makes of car fighting for the lead. The Fordwater Trophy race was for closed cars and Stirling Moss

"…and someone's brakes have failed at Woodcote"

There are always some interesting pieces of non-competing machinery to be found in the paddock on race weekends. A rather handsome Jaguar XK140…

was driving a DB4GT, whereas Roy Salvadori was in a 3.8 Jaguar. They were in close company for most of the 10 laps and accompanied by Jack Sears, also driving a 3.8 Jag.

They finished in that order and towards the end of the race Moss managed to pull away from the other two, probably because Salvadori had his work cut out fending off Jack Sears. Twenty-eight seconds separated them over the line.

The Whitsun Meeting of 1960 was very much the mixture as before. Mostly sports cars, one race for closed cars and the race for pre-war racing cars. It got off the mark with a race for the Cibie Cup. This was over ten laps for the smaller closed production cars.

It was great fun to watch and as the cars were considerably slower than most of those seen on this track, a detailed study could be made of them as they went by.

First three across the line were a brace of Austin A40s and a Borgward Isabella. The drivers were Gaston, Lawrence, and Blydenstein.

Second race of the day was the now customary *Autosport* Series Race for production sports cars. This also was great fun to watch, with a wide variety of makes and amateur drivers in the true sense of the word. Understandably the more powerful cars tended to be at the front by the end of the race, but it

was exciting to watch how they got there. First to the line was a big Austin Healey 3000 with a 3.4 Jaguar close on his heels, only two seconds between them. In third place was a Lotus Elite. The drivers: Sutton, Sargent, and Hurrell.

Event 3, the Whitsun Trophy, was 21 laps for sports cars (of the specialist kind). This, once again, was a duel between Cooper and Lotus. A Cooper-Monaco was the victor but with a couple of Lotus-Climax 15 s second and third. By the end of this race the entire field was quite strung out and the back markers several laps down. Tom Dickson won from Doug Graham and Chris Martyn.

… and a very desirable Bristol 405.

Graham Hill

The Goodwood crowd did not see Graham Hill race until the late 1950s. At the Easter meeting of 1957 he drove a Connaught entered by C.T. Atkins in the 12-lap Formula 2 race for the Lavant Cup. He got onto the second row of the grid for the start but did not feature in the results. At the September meeting that year he drove a works Lotus–Climax sports car in the 21-lap race for the Goodwood Trophy.

In the Formula 2 Lavant Cup race on Easter Monday 1958 he finished in second place driving a works Lotus–Climax behind Jack Brabham in a Cooper–Climax. In 1959 he drove for Lotus again, but by 1960 he was with BRM and finished fifth in the Formula 1 42-lap International "100" for the Glover Trophy at the Easter meeting. Later that year he drove a 1600 cc Porsche in the 25th RAC Tourist Trophy race and finished fourth. He was a great driver to watch through the corners, determination written all over his face.

Easter Monday 30th March 1959—Madgwick
Goodwood International "100" for the Glover Trophy, 42 laps, Formula 1.
Graham Hill in the new works Lotus-Climax.
[Race winner: Stirling Moss (Cooper-Climax T51).]

Chapter 14

Philip Fotheringham-Parker driving ERA R5B (Remus) finished fourth in the 1951 Second Easter Handicap. This ex Bira car was owned and raced jointly by Philip Fotheringham-Parker and Duncan Hamilton from 1951 to 1954.

Another step back in time

A great deal of noise heralded the warming up of the cars for the next race. This was the ten-lap contest between the pre-war racing cars. It proved to be third time lucky for J. Goodhew and his wonderful ERA-Delage. In 1958 he had finished second in this event and in 1959 he was third, but this year he took the chequered flag to win by over three seconds from Gordon Chapman in his ERA R2A. Third place was taken by Keith Schellenberg and his fantastic Barnato-Hassan Bentley.

I had seen Keith Schellenberg drive this car before and he always drove it with the enthusiasm and exuberance and in the manner to which he was convinced that it was accustomed.

Each one of these three cars has quite a history and there is not enough room within these pages to do justice to any of them. However, a bit of background information may help the reader.

The chassis of J. Goodhew's ERA-Delage dates back to 1926 when several were built as 1½ litre racing cars by Delage. In 1927 they were very successful in Grand Prix racing around Europe, winning both the French and Italian races and placed second or third in several others.

One was rebuilt by the famous Italian racing driver and later, mechanic to Scuderia Ferrari, Giulio Ramponi, for Dick Seaman to race in 1936. His successes that year with this car included the Prix de Berne and the RAC Light Car Race on the Isle of Man. It was after World War II that the ERA engine was installed, as spare parts for the original Delage unit were almost non-existent. It was then owned for a time by Rob Walker and driven extensively by Tony Rolt with good results. On one occasion Roy Salvadori drove it into second place in a 14-mile race at Crystal Palace. J. Goodhew used it regularly after buying it and had his share of success with what was by then a "Vintage" car.

Gordon Chapman's ERA R2A dates back to 1934 and was only the second ERA ever built. It was raced during 1934 and 1935 by Humphry Cook and Raymond Mays, who, with Peter Berthon, had formed the ERA Company in 1933. In 1936 it was sold to Nicky Embiricos and was raced by him and A. Pollock until August 1939.

In 1947 it was bought by George Abecassis and raced by him, John Heath, and others. Gordon Chapman bought it in the spring of 1958 and raced it extensively until the end of 1963 with great success. Even after selling it he would still drive this wonderful machine on occasions in VSCC historic events.

Easter Monday 22nd April 1957
Sussex Trophy, 21-lap race for larger sports cars—Madgwick.
Archie Scott-Brown driving the works Lister-Jaguar won from Roy Salvadori in the works Aston Martin DBR1 (second) and Tony Brooks in the works DB3S (third).
In this race Archie Scott-Brown set a new sports car lap record at 91.33 mph.

"Why are all those men waving flags along a quiet road like this?"

The Barnato-Hassan Bentley was built in 1934 by Walter Hassan for Woolf Barnarto for use in Brooklands Outer Circuit races and for record breaking. Known as the Barnato-Hassan Special it was originally fitted with a 6½-litre Speed Six Bentley engine taken from Barnato's road racing car, but in 1935 this was replaced with an 8-litre unit and the car was then raced by Oliver Bertram. Already a successful Brooklands driver with many different cars including the well known 10½-litre Delage, Bertram raced the Barnato-Hassan Special regularly and was involved in record breaking until the outbreak of war in 1939. In August 1936 he had completed a flying lap round the outer circuit at 142.60 mph and established a new outright record. Unfortunately he was not to hold it for long, as on 7th October John Cobb, driving his famous Napier-Railton, put in a lap at 143.44 mph which stands to this day.

The "Marque" Sports Car Race (10 laps) at the 1960 meeting contained a good collection of interesting machinery circulating at speed and producing a few hairy moments. These races contain as much excitement towards the back of the field as at the front. None of the back markers wished to be too far back at the finish and would do anything to stay as far up the field as they could, even if the car behind them was faster than they were. It was nice to see variety at the flag. The winner was Hextall driving a Triumph TR2, second was McCowen in an AC-Bristol, and third, Turner in a big Austin Healey 3000.

Final race of the day was the ten-lap Whitsun Handicap. Always exciting to see how the "scratch" man carved his way through the field; this one did not disappoint. The early cars doing their best to stay up front and those more heavily handicapped trying hard to beat them. Chris Kerrison won in his Lotus-Climax 11, eight seconds ahead of Tom Dickson's Cooper-Climax T49 who had Ken Yeates' Lister-Bristol snapping at his heels. G

The Goodwood International "100" for the Glover Trophy

42-lap scratch race for Grand Prix Cars

A pair of BRMs

Harry Schell and Jo Bonnier. They finished third and fourth behind Stirling Moss (first) in Rob Walker's Cooper-Climax and Jack Brabham (second) in a works Cooper-Climax.

Jack Fairman had a day out in the Scuderia Centro-Sud Maserati 250F.

126

Glover Trophy

Bruce McLaren

Works 2208 cc Cooper-Climax.

The Fordwater Trophy

10-lap scratch race for non-supercharged saloon cars.

Jags to the fore. Just after the start, the cars approaching Madgwick.

As they take Madgwick

With the leaders already into Fordwater, the tailenders do their best to get round Madgwick corner without incident.

Race result:
1 Ivor Bueb (Equipe Endeavour Jaguar 3.4)
2 Roy Salvadori (John Coombs Racing Jaguar 3.4)
3 Sir Gawaine Baillie (privately entered Jaguar 3.4)

Jim Clark

This talented and highly respected driver arrived on the Goodwood scene at the very end of the period covered by this book. He drove an Ecurie Ecosse Tojeiro-Jaguar in the 1959 Tourist Trophy race, which was crashed by his co-driver after Clark had been doing very well with it.

In 1960 he won the Formula Junior Chichester Cup driving a Lotus-Ford 18 at the Easter meeting and then, at the TT meeting in August, with the same car he won the seven-lap heat and finished second in the 21-lap final of the BARC Formula Junior Championship race. A clear sign of things to come.

5th September 1959—Fordwater
24th RAC Tourist Trophy Race over six hours.
Jim Clark driving the Ecurie Ecosse Tojeiro-Jaguar. This car was doing well until crashed by co-driver Masten Gregory. Race winner was the Aston Martin DBR1 driven by Carroll Shelby, Jack Fairman, and Stirling Moss.

Chapter 15

Silver Jubilee RAC Tourist Trophy—20th August 1960. Stirling Moss on his way to victory for the sixth time, on this occasion driving Rob Walker's 250GT Ferrari Berlinetta.

The end of an era

For the 25th RAC Tourist Trophy, a different format was hatched up. The Silver Jubilee race was shorter than in previous years and was for closed cars. Also, there was a programme of Formula Junior races, which preceded it. These were for the BARC Formula Junior Championship and

comprised two seven-lap heats and a 21-lap final.

These events, with very evenly matched cars, always showed the spectator who the best drivers were.

In Heat 1, Trevor Taylor driving a Lotus-Ford 18 won in convincing style by almost ten seconds from Dick Prior driving a Lola-Ford Mk2 who, in turn, was almost eight seconds ahead of Cliff Johnson in another Lotus-Ford 18.

Heat 2 was a much closer affair, with a masterly display of driving by a young Jim Clark in a Lotus-Ford 18, who just managed to stay in front of Mike McKee in a similar car. Just one second separating them as they crossed the line. Third was Peter Ashdown in a Lola-Ford Mk2.

The final was quite nail biting for the spectator. There were several groups of cars, all evenly matched, travelling at speed very close together. The standard of driving by all was of the highest. We were constantly expecting them to touch and come to grief. There were a few incidents among those further back, but the leading pack kept us on our toes throughout. It was Trevor Taylor's day and he crossed the line just three seconds ahead of Jim Clark with Mike McKee in third place.

Trevor Taylor and Jim Clark put in identical laps at 92.50 mph to set a new record for Formula Junior.

Then came the main event, the 25th race for the Tourist Trophy. A three-hour race, it was filled with action and excitement in the early stages but punctures and mechanical problems spread the field out and Stirling Moss, driving Rob Walker's 250GT Ferrari, won by two laps. This was a hat trick for him at Goodwood and his sixth TT win overall.

Roy Salvadori, who finished second driving one of John Ogier's Aston Martin DB4GTs, had pushed Moss very hard in the early stages of the race and was one of the puncture sufferers. Though he got back into second place after his pit stop when Innes Ireland's Ogier DB4 had some mechanical problems, Moss was just too far away by then.

Innes Ireland and Sir John Whitmore managed to get their ailing Aston Martin into third place ahead of Graham Hill's Porsche 1600GS. Fourth place earned Hill the first prize in the 2-litre class. Fifth place was taken by Graham Whitehead and Jack Fairman driving a Ferrari 250GT SWB and sixth was Colin Davis in yet another Ferrari 250GT SWB. The 1100 cc class was filled entirely by Lotus Elites, 11 of them in all and was won by Peter Lumsden and Chris Kerrison.

There was no real pressure on Moss for the second half of the race and he cruised to victory. However, he did set the fastest lap at 89.44 mph, a new GT record, which proves that he was not hanging about. He would go on to win his seventh Tourist Trophy at Goodwood in 1961. This he achieved to a great extent by his smooth driving style. He was not only faster than the rest but also kinder to his tyres. Some of the opposition's cars lacked grip towards the end of the race and extra pit stops were needed.

The sights, sounds, and smells of the Goodwood motor circuit will be with me always. Stored away in the old memory box are the exploits of all the great drivers mentioned, as well as some which, through lack of space, are not. The unmistakable voice of the enthusiastic and effervescent John Bolster over the public address system was part of that "Goodwood experience" in the early days.

I have followed motor racing ever since and there have been many great drivers, many fantastic achievements in many marvellous races over the years but, for me, nothing will quite compare to those years spent in the enclosures and paddock at Goodwood: 1948 to 1960 were truly the golden years.

Following yet another very enjoyable meeting, I remember we made our way out of the enclosure and across the road towards the car park. Once again the air was filled with the sound of people talking in happy mood, discussing the events of the day; the good fortune for some drivers and the misfortune for others. Light-hearted chatter between friends and complete strangers, resolving to make a note on the calendar at home of the date of the next meeting.

Once again, we entered the car park and the crowd dispersed. Each small group making off towards their own particular vehicles.

"Ah! Now! Where did we park the car?"

Then, some ten minutes or so later...

"Are you sure we left it in this car park?" G

Postscript

The re-introduction of the rear-engined racing car by Cooper (remember the Auto Union) and its development into a highly-successful Formula 1 winner, swiftly followed by Lotus and others, heralded a new era in motor racing. Aerodynamics became the name of the game and each new season saw a fresh collection from the drawing boards. This meant that the driver gradually disappeared from view within the bodywork.

Throughout the 1960s speeds were ever increasing and the overall excitement of motor racing was still great, but the sheer spectacle of watching the drivers fighting with proper size steering wheels as the sometimes unwieldy machines went from understeer to oversteer and back again was gone for ever. So too was the thrill of seeing the masters at work, holding powerful and awe-inspiring machines in beautiful four-wheel drifts at incredible speeds.

It was a very sad day in 1966 when the Goodwood gates closed for the last time. But maybe it was fate taking a hand so that this unique circuit could be held in a "time-warp" until 1998 when it re-opened. What a *blast from the past* that was! Now, thanks to Lord March and his team of keen and dedicated assistants, we can enjoy once more the sights, sounds, and smells of a bygone era. Narrow tyres, engines in the right place, "well most of the time", and, above all, being able to see the drivers at work. Fabulous cars being driven by fantastic drivers "some old, many not so old" with all the verve and enthusiasm that was witnessed all those years ago. Now, each year for the Revival Meetings, spectators and participants travel from all the corners of the globe for the magic of the "Goodwood Experience". Many of the competing cars do likewise and it is just great to see them all.

I am so glad that I was born when I was and that in 1948 and beyond, I lived just a short bicycle ride from one of the most exciting motor sport venues in England, which has become the best of its kind in the world. Long may it continue. G

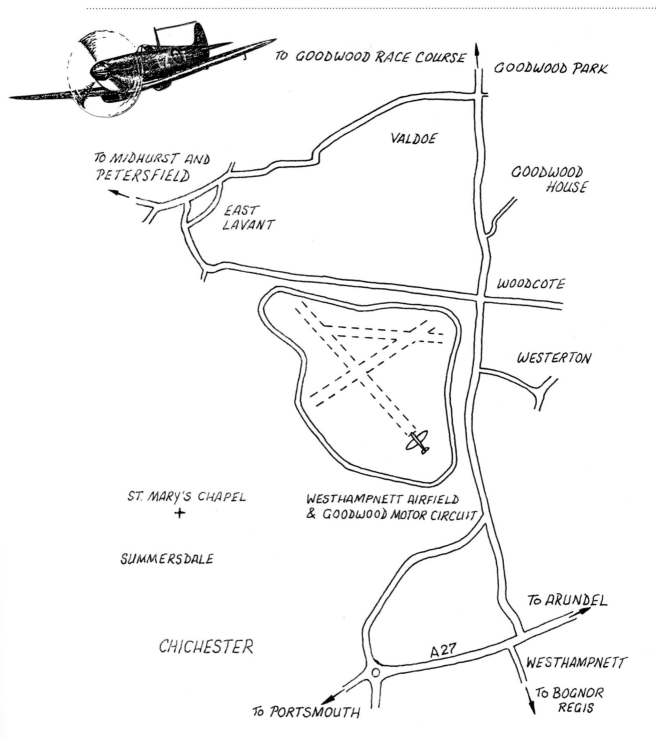

TO GOODWOOD RACE COURSE

GOODWOOD PARK

VALDOE

TO MIDHURST AND PETERSFIELD

GOODWOOD HOUSE

EAST LAVANT

WOODCOTE

WESTERTON

ST. MARY'S CHAPEL
+

WESTHAMPNETT AIRFIELD & GOODWOOD MOTOR CIRCUIT

SUMMERSDALE

TO ARUNDEL

CHICHESTER

A27

WESTHAMPNETT

TO BOGNOR REGIS

TO PORTSMOUTH

How to find the Goodwood Motor Circuit in 1948

Appendix: BARC Programme Pages

This appendix is a compilation of, what I believe are, interesting pages taken from the BARC Goodwood Motor Racing Programmes for the events held at the circuit between September 1949 and Easter 1959. Permission for these to be included in this book has been granted by the BARC (British Automobile Racing Club), for which I am most grateful. I believe that they add dimension to my recollections of the events which I, and countless others, so greatly enjoyed at that time.

As mentioned at the beginning of this book, I attended most Motor Race Meetings held at Goodwood between September 1948 and May 1966 and have most of the Programmes still in reasonable condition. A few are showing signs that the occasion was rather damp and sadly, through the passage of time, some have gone missing, probably through being retrieved from the loft for some reason or other and then not put back with their friends.

Looking at them again, after all these years, I find them fascinating as well as historically interesting. I hope that readers of all ages will do likewise.

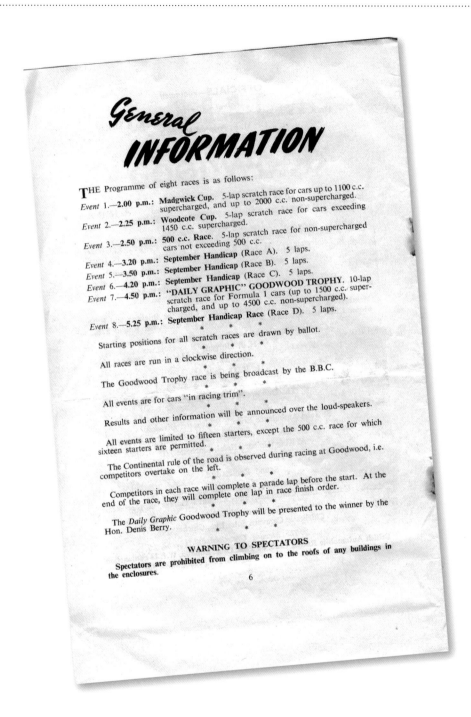

General INFORMATION

THE Programme of eight races is as follows:

Event 1.—2.00 p.m.: **Madgwick Cup.** 5-lap scratch race for cars up to 1100 c.c. supercharged, and up to 2000 c.c. non-supercharged.

Event 2.—2.25 p.m.: **Woodcote Cup.** 5-lap scratch race for cars exceeding 1450 c.c. supercharged.

Event 3.—2.50 p.m.: **500 c.c. Race.** 5-lap scratch race for non-supercharged cars not exceeding 500 c.c.

Event 4.—3.20 p.m.: **September Handicap** (Race A). 5 laps.

Event 5.—3.50 p.m.: **September Handicap** (Race B). 5 laps.

Event 6.—4.20 p.m.: **September Handicap** (Race C). 5 laps.

Event 7.—4.50 p.m.: **"DAILY GRAPHIC" GOODWOOD TROPHY.** 10-lap scratch race for Formula 1 cars (up to 1500 c.c. supercharged, and up to 4500 c.c. non-supercharged).

Event 8.—5.25 p.m.: **September Handicap Race** (Race D). 5 laps.

* * *

Starting positions for all scratch races are drawn by ballot.

* * *

All races are run in a clockwise direction.

* * *

The Goodwood Trophy race is being broadcast by the B.B.C.

* * *

All events are for cars "in racing trim".

* * *

Results and other information will be announced over the loud-speakers.

* * *

All events are limited to fifteen starters, except the 500 c.c. race for which sixteen starters are permitted.

* * *

The Continental rule of the road is observed during racing at Goodwood, i.e. competitors overtake on the left.

* * *

Competitors in each race will complete a parade lap before the start. At the end of the race, they will complete one lap in race finish order.

* * *

The *Daily Graphic* Goodwood Trophy will be presented to the winner by the Hon. Denis Berry.

* * *

WARNING TO SPECTATORS

Spectators are prohibited from climbing on to the roofs of any buildings in the enclosures.

6

Perhaps the last sentence on this page from 17th September 1949 was precipitated by the actions of myself and a few others at the first meeting one year earlier. See page 2.

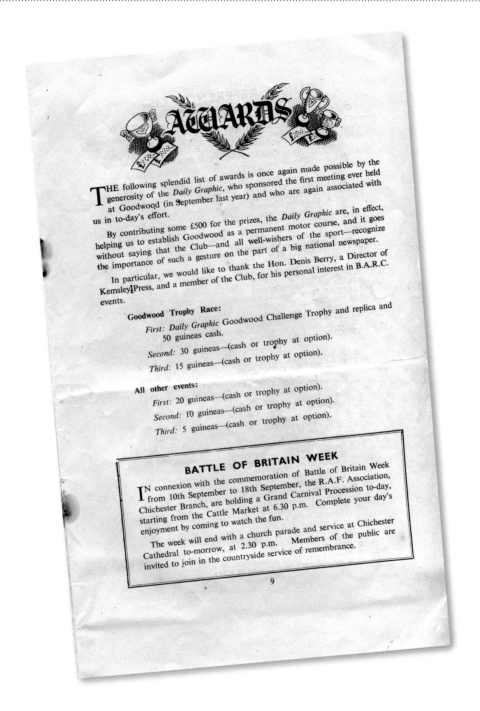

AWARDS

THE following splendid list of awards is once again made possible by the generosity of the *Daily Graphic*, who sponsored the first meeting ever held at Goodwood (in September last year) and who are again associated with us in to-day's effort.

By contributing some £500 for the prizes, the *Daily Graphic* are, in effect, helping us to establish Goodwood as a permanent motor course, and it goes without saying that the Club—and all well-wishers of the sport—recognize the importance of such a gesture on the part of a big national newspaper.

In particular, we would like to thank the Hon. Denis Berry, a Director of Kemsley Press, and a member of the Club, for his personal interest in B.A.R.C. events.

Goodwood Trophy Race:

First: *Daily Graphic* Goodwood Challenge Trophy and replica and 50 guineas cash.

Second: 30 guineas—(cash or trophy at option).

Third: 15 guineas—(cash or trophy at option).

All other events:

First: 20 guineas—(cash or trophy at option).

Second: 10 guineas—(cash or trophy at option).

Third: 5 guineas—(cash or trophy at option).

BATTLE OF BRITAIN WEEK

IN connexion with the commemoration of Battle of Britain Week from 10th September to 18th September, the R.A.F. Association, Chichester Branch, are holding a Grand Carnival Procession to-day, starting from the Cattle Market at 6.30 p.m. Complete your day's enjoyment by coming to watch the fun.

The week will end with a church parade and service at Chichester Cathedral to-morrow, at 2.30 p.m. Members of the public are invited to join in the countryside service of remembrance.

9

The financial rewards available in those days are unbelievable compared to the twenty-first century and are quoted in guineas (£1-1-0) or £1.05p. This page from 17th September 1949.

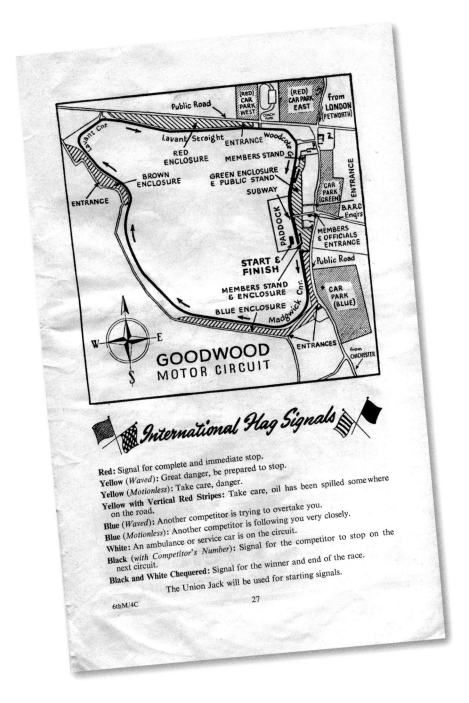

International Flag Signals

Red: Signal for complete and immediate stop.

Yellow (*Waved*): Great danger, be prepared to stop.

Yellow (*Motionless*): Take care, danger.

Yellow with Vertical Red Stripes: Take care, oil has been spilled somewhere on the road.

Blue (*Waved*): Another competitor is trying to overtake you.

Blue (*Motionless*): Another competitor is following you very closely.

White: An ambulance or service car is on the circuit.

Black (*with Competitor's Number*): Signal for the competitor to stop on the next circuit.

Black and White Chequered: Signal for the winner and end of the race.

The Union Jack will be used for starting signals.

6thM/4C   27

This map of the circuit from near the centre of the BARC programme for the "International Goodwood Motor Race Meeting 30th September 1950" shows how little has changed over the years. The list of flag signals below could have come from a recent programme.

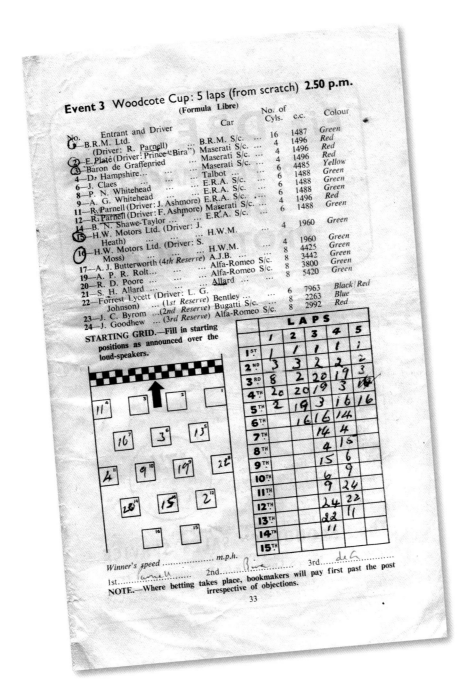

Event 3 Woodcote Cup: 5 laps (from scratch) **2.50 p.m.**

(Formula Libre)

No.	Entrant and Driver	Car	No. of Cyls.	c.c.	Colour
1	B.R.M. Ltd. (Driver: R. Parnell)	B.R.M. S/c	16	1487	Green
2	E. Platé (Driver: Prince "Bira")	Maserati S/c	4	1496	Red
3	Baron de Graffenried	Maserati S/c	4	1496	Red
4	D. Hampshire	Maserati S/c	4	1496	Yellow
6	J. Claes	Talbot	6	4485	Green
8	P. N. Whitehead	E.R.A. S/c	6	1488	Green
9	A. G. Whitehead	E.R.A. S/c	6	1488	Green
11	R. Parnell (Driver: J. Ashmore)	E.R.A. S/c	6	1488	Green
12	R. Parnell (Driver: F. Ashmore)	Maserati S/c	4	1496	Red
14	B. N. Shawe-Taylor	E.R.A. S/c	6	1488	Green
15	H.W. Motors Ltd. (Driver: J. Heath)	H.W.M.	4	1960	Green
16	H.W. Motors Ltd. (Driver: S. Moss)	H.W.M.	4	1960	Green
17	A. J. Butterworth (4th Reserve)	A.J.B.	8	4425	Green
19	A. P. R. Rolt	Alfa-Romeo S/c	8	3442	Green
20	R. D. Poore	Alfa-Romeo S/c	8	3800	Green
21	S. H. Allard	Allard	8	5420	Green
22	Forrest Lycett (Driver: L. G. Johnson) ... (1st Reserve)	Bentley	6	7963	Black/Red
23	J. C. Byrom ...(2nd Reserve)	Bugatti S/c	8	2263	Blue
24	J. Goodhew ...(3rd Reserve)	Alfa-Romeo S/c	8	2992	Red

STARTING GRID.—Fill in starting positions as announced over the loud-speakers.

	LAPS				
	1	**2**	**3**	**4**	**5**
1ST	1	1	1	1	1
2ND	3	3	2	2	2
3RD	8	2	20	19	3
4TH	20	20	19	3	19
5TH	2	19	3	16	16
6TH		16	16	14	
7TH			14	4	
8TH			4	15	
9TH			15	6	
10TH			6	9	
11TH			9	24	
12TH			24	22	
13TH			22	11	
14TH			11		
15TH					

Winner's speed .... m.p.h.

1st... *Parnell* ...... 2nd... *Bira* ...... 3rd... *de G* ......

NOTE.—Where betting takes place, bookmakers will pay first past the post irrespective of objections.

33

The list of entries and lap chart from the BARC programme of 30th September 1950 on the occasion of the V16 BRM winning its first race at Goodwood in the hands of Reg Parnell, and in the pouring rain. B. Bira came from the back of the grid to finish second in the 4CLT Maserati in just five laps.

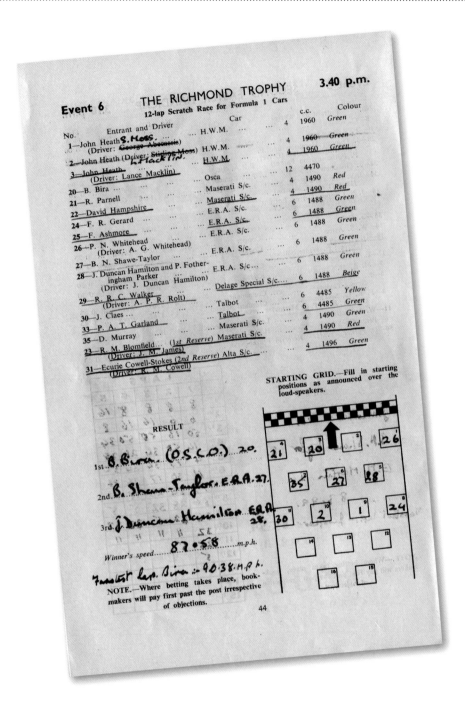

These two pages tell the story of the Richmond Trophy Race of 26th March 1951. Formula 1 then being 4½ litre or 1½ litre supercharged. Moss and Macklin did well to finish fifth and seventh in their 2 litre HWMs from Row 3 of the grid.

Britain's greatest motoring event!

INTERNATIONAL

DAILY EXPRESS
TROPHY MEETING
SILVERSTONE

SATURDAY, MAY 5th

'All-in' Car Ticket booked in advance 25/- (on the day 30/-). Admits car and ALL passengers. South and North Grand Stands 21/- per seat. Cars 10/- extra. Tickets from DAILY EXPRESS Trophy Office, Fleet Street, London, E.C.4.

Organised by the B.R.D.C.

	L A P S											
	1	**2**	**3**	**4**	**5**	**6**	**7**	**8**	**9**	**10**	**11**	**12**
1ST.	20	20	20	20	20	20	20	20	20	20	20	20
2ND.	21	27	27	21	27	27	27	27	27	27	27	27
3RD.	27	28	21	27	27	28	36	30	30	28	28	28
4TH.	28	21	28	28	28	30	28	28	28	30	30	30
5TH.	30	30	30	30	30	1	1	1	1	1	1	1
6TH.		2	1	1	1	2	2	2	2	2	2	26
7TH.		26	2	2	2	26	26	26	26	26	26	2
8TH.		1	26	26	26							
9TH.		24	24									
10TH.												
11TH.												
12TH.												
13TH.												
14TH.												
15TH.												

45

COMPETITION NUMBERS, ENTRANTS, CARS, ENGINE DATA, AND DRIVERS

No.	Entrant	Car	Colour	No. of Cyls.	Bore and Stroke in m.m.	c.c.	Driver (1)	Driver (2)	No.
							Cars with Engines over 3000 c.c. capacity:		
1—W. Lyons	Jaguar XK120C	Green	6	83 x 106	3442	Stirling Moss	P. Walker	1
2—W. Lyons	Jaguar XK120C	Green	6	83 x 106	3442	A. P. R. Rolt	J. Duncan Hamilton	2
3—W. Lyons	Jaguar XK120C	Green	6	83 x 106	3442	P. N. Whitehead	I. M. M. Stewart	3
4—Vaino Hollming	Jaguar XK120	Silver	6	83 x 106	3442	Vaino Hollming	Roger Laurent	4
5—Ecurie Ecosse	Jaguar XK120C	Green	6	83 x 106	3442	Sir J. Scott Douglas	Sora Duntov	5
7—S. H. Allard	Allard	Green	8	97 x 92	5420	A. Hume	G. E. Thomas	7
8—F. G. Curtis	Allard	Green	8	97 x 92	5420	F. G. Curtis	J. E. G. Fairman	8
9—P. Levegh	Talbot	Blue	6	93 x 110	4483	P. Levegh	P. Etancelin	9
10—J. B. Swift	Jaguar XK120	Green	6	83 x 106	3442	J. B. Swift	C. Heath	10
11—S. J. Boshier	Jaguar XK120	Black	6	83 x 106	3442	S. J. Boshier	W. B. Black	11
Reserve							Reserve: L. Wood	
14—J. Goodhew	Lagonda	Red	6	88 x 120	4467	J. Goodhew	R. F. Wright	14
							Reserve: W. Rider	
							Cars with Engines over 1500 c.c. and up to 3000 c.c.:		
15—David Brown	Aston Martin DB3	Green	6	83 x 90	2922	R. Parnell	E. Thompson	15
16—David Brown	Aston Martin DB3	Green	6	78 x 90	2580	G. Abecassis	R. D. Poore	16
17—David Brown	Aston Martin DB3	Green	6	78 x 90	2580	P. Collins	P. W. C. Griffith	17
18—M. F. L. Falkner	Aston Martin DB2	Grey	6	78 x 90	2580	M. F. L. Falkner	T. G. Clarke	18
								Reserve: I. P. B. Denton	
19—G. Caprara	Ferrari	Red	12	70 x 59	2715	R. Baird	R. F. Salvadori	19
							Reserve: D. J. Griffin	
20—T. Cole	Ferrari	Blue	12	70 x 59	2715	T. Cole	A. G. Whitehead	20
21—F. R. Gerard	Frazer-Nash	Green/Cream	6	66 x 96	1971	F. R. Gerard	D. A. Clarke	21
							Reserve: R. M. Turner	
22—H. A. Mitchell	Frazer-Nash	Green	6	66 x 96	1971	H. A. Mitchell	P. Scott-Russell	22
23—J. R. Stoop	Frazer-Nash	Green	6	66 x 96	1971	J. R. Stoop	P. S. Wilson	23
25—T. M. Meyer	H.W.M.	Green	4	83 x 90	1960	T. M. Meyer	P. Fotheringham-Parker	25
26—W. D. R. Lamb	Healey	Green	4	80 x 120	2443	W. D. R. Lamb	E. P. Going	26
27—D. S. Boston	Healey	Green	4	80 x 120	2443	D. S. Boston	R. G. Shattock	27
28—S. G. Greene	Frazer-Nash	Green	6	66 x 96	1971	T. A. D. Crook	R. W. Jacobs	28
Reserves									
30—E. B. Wadsworth (1st)	Healey	Chrome	4	80 x 120	2443	E. B. Wadsworth	G. H. Beetson	30
								Reserve: J. R. Brown	
31—J. Beckwith-Smith (2nd)	Frazer-Nash B.M.W.	Green	6	66 x 96	1971	J. Beckwith-Smith	S. C. Gibbs	31
							Cars with Engines up to 1500 c.c. capacity:		
32—The Monkey Stable	Lester M.G.	Green	4	72 x 90	1467	J. C. C. Mayers	M. J. Keen	32
33—The Monkey Stable	Lester M.G.	Green	4	72 x 90	1467	G. A. Ruddock	R. F. Peacock	33
34—The Monkey Stable	Lester M.G.	Green	4	72 x 90	1467	L. Leston	T. Line	34
35—F. C. Davis	Cooper M.G.	Silver	4	73 x 90	1496	F. C. Davis	J. Coombs	35
36—L. Leonard	Cooper M.G.	Silver	4	73 x 90	1496	L. Leonard	D. Annable	36
37—L. Gibbs	H.R.G.	Green	4	68 x 103	1496	L. Gibbs	A. S. Heal	37
38—J. Kelly	Jowett Jupiter	Bronze	4	72 x 90	1486	J. Kelly	L. Gill	38
								Reserve: H. Sullivan	
Reserves									
39—D. M. D. Blakely (1st)	H.R.G.	Green	4	68 x 103	1496	D. M. D. Blakely	A. S. Findlater	39
40—G. E. Phillips (2nd)	M.G. (TD.)	Green	4	66 x 90	1250	G. E. Phillips	A. C. Rippon	40
41—T. W. Dargue (3rd)	M.G. Special	Green	4	72 x 90	1467	T. W. Dargue	E. J. Haesendonck	41
42—E. W. Cuff Miller (4th)	Jowett Jupiter	Green	4	72 x 90	1486	E. W. Cuff Miller	G. Dudley	42

The list of entrants, cars, and drivers for the first Nine-hour race at Goodwood on 16th August 1952. Starting at 3pm and ending at midnight. An experience not to be forgotten.

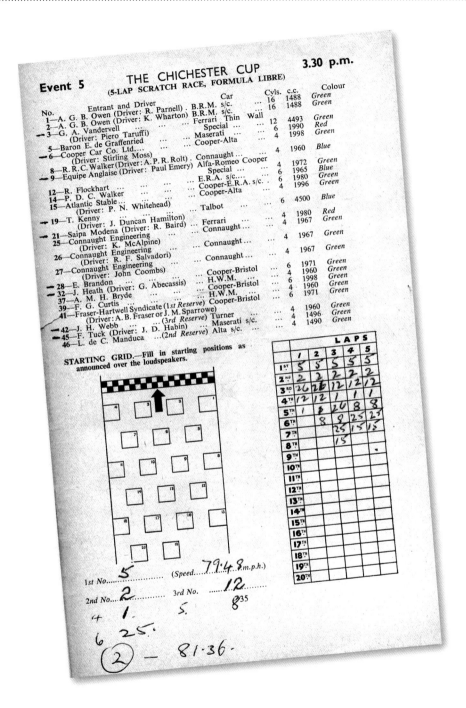

Event 5 THE CHICHESTER CUP **3.30 p.m.**
(5-LAP SCRATCH RACE, FORMULA LIBRE)

No.	Entrant and Driver	Car	Cyls.	c.c.	Colour
1—A. G. B. Owen (Driver: R. Parnell)	B.R.M. s/c	16	1488	Green
2—A. G. B. Owen (Driver: K. Wharton)	B.R.M. s/c	16	1488	Green
3—G. A. Vandervell (Driver: Piero Taruffi)	Ferrari Thin Wall Special	12	4493	Green
5—Baron E. de Graffenried	Maserati	6	1990	Red
6—Cooper Car Co. Ltd. (Driver: Stirling Moss)	Cooper-Alta	4	1998	Green
8—R. R. C. Walker (Driver: A. P. R. Rolt)	Connaught	4	1960	Blue
9—Equipe Anglaise (Driver: Paul Emery)	Alfa-Romeo Cooper Special	4	1972	Green
12—R. Flockhart	E.R.A. s/c	6	1965	Blue
14—P. D. C. Walker	Cooper-E.R.A. s/c	6	1980	Green
15—Atlantic Stable (Driver: P. N. Whitehead)	Cooper-Alta	4	1996	Green
19—T. Kenny	Talbot	6	4500	Blue
21—Saipa Modena (Driver: J. Duncan Hamilton)	Ferrari	4	1980	Red
25—Connaught Engineering (Driver: R. Baird)	Connaught	4	1967	Green
26—Connaught Engineering (Driver: K. McAlpine)	Connaught	4	1967	Green
27—Connaught Engineering (Driver: R. F. Salvadori)	Connaught	4	1967	Green
28—E. Brandon (Driver: John Coombs)	Cooper-Bristol	6	1971	Green
32—J. Heath (Driver: G. Abecassis)	H.W.M.	4	1960	Green
37—A. M. H. Bryde	Cooper-Bristol	6	1998	Green
39—F. G. Curtis	H.W.M.	4	1960	Green
41—Fraser-Hartwell Syndicate (1st Reserve) (Driver: A. B. Fraser or J. M. Sparrowe)	Cooper-Bristol	6	1971	Green
42—J. H. Webb (3rd Reserve)	Turner	4	1960	Green
45—F. Tuck (Driver: J. D. Habin)	Maserati s/c	4	1496	Green
46—L. de C. Manduca (2nd Reserve)	Alta s/c	4	1490	Green

STARTING GRID.—Fill in starting positions as announced over the loudspeakers.

LAPS	1	2	3	4	5
1ST	5	5	5	5	5
2ND	2	2	2	2	2
3RD	26	26	12	12	12
4TH	12	12	1	1	1
5TH	1	8	26	8	8
6TH		8	8	25	25
7TH			25	15	15
8TH			15		
9TH					
10TH					
11TH					
12TH					
13TH					
14TH					
15TH					
16TH					
17TH					
18TH					
19TH					
20TH					

1st No. 5 (Speed 79·48 m.p.h.)

2nd No. 2   3rd No. 12

4 1. 5. 8·35

6 25.

② — 81·36.

The list of cars and drivers for the Chichester Cup race of 6th April 1953. This is typical of the events we enjoyed so much at Goodwood in the 1950s. Those marked "—" are believed to be non-starters.

EVENT 5

GOODWOOD TROPHY

3.47 p.m.

15 laps (from scratch) (Formula Libre)

No.	Entrant and Driver	Car	No. of Cyls.	c.c.	Colour
1	A. G. B. Owen (Driver: J. M. Fangio)	B.R.M. s/c.	16	1488	Green
2	A. G. B. Owen (Driver: K. Wharton)	B.R.M. s/c.	16	1488	Green
3	A. G. B. Owen (Driver: to be nominated)	B.R.M. s/c.	16	1488	Green
4	G. A. Vandervell (Driver: J. M. Hawthorn)	Ferrari Thin Wall Special	4	4493	Green
5	O. Volonterio	Maserati	4	1984	Red
6	W. Sturzebecher	Meteor-Veritas	6	1998	Silver
7	Cooper Car Co. (Driver: Stirling Moss)	Cooper-Alta	4	1960	Green
8	F. R. Gerard	Cooper-Bristol	6	1971	Green/Cream
9	The Border Reivers (Driver: J. Somervail or J. K. Hall)	Cooper-Bristol	6	1971	Blue
10	Connaught Engineering (Driver: R. Salvadori)	Connaught	4	1967	Green
11	R. R. C. Walker (Driver: A. P. R. Rolt)	Connaught	4	1960	Blue
12	L. Marr	Connaught	4	1960	Green
14	Ecurie Britannique (Driver: G. Jason-Henry)	Connaught	4	1960	Green
15	H. W. Motors (Driver: L. Macklin)	H.W.M.	4	1991	Green
16	Emeryson Cars (Driver: P. Emery)	Emeryson	6	1488	Green
17	A. G. Whitehead	E.R.A. s/c.	6	1980	Blue
18	R. Flockhart	E.R.A. s/c.	6	1488	Blue
19	The Border Reivers (Driver: J. R. McBain or J. Somervail)	R.R.A. s/c.	6	1781	Green
20	G. N. Richardson (1st Reserve)	Cooper-Bristol	6	1971	Green
21	Goulds Garage (Driver: H. Gould) (2nd Reserve)	Cooper-Bristol	6	1971	Green
22	R. J. Chase (Driver: J. Duncan Hamilton)	Cooper-Bristol	6	1971	

24

The lap chart for the Goodwood Trophy of 26th September 1953 looks as if the race might have lacked excitement. But far from it. The spectators were kept on their toes throughout the 15 laps and the pre-war ERAs were still a match for the modern machinery. Those with numbers crossed "/" are believed to be non-starters.

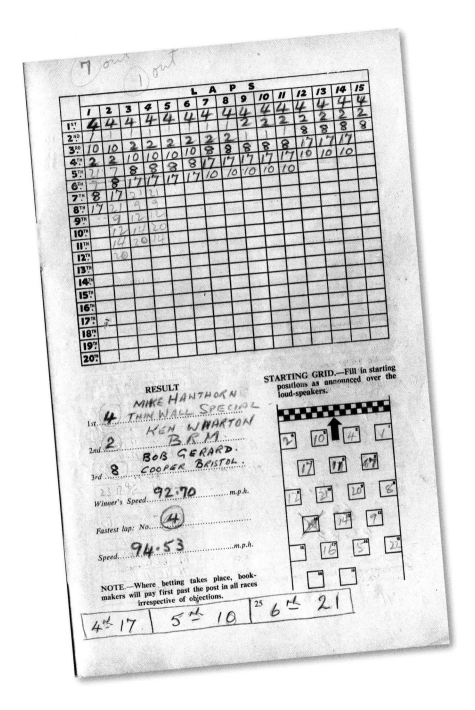

7 out   1 out

L A P S

	1	2	3	4	5	6	7	8	9	10	11	12	13	14	15
1ST	4	4	4	4	4	4	4	4	4 / 2	4 / 2	4 / 2	4 / 2	4 / 2	4 / 2	4 / 2
2ND			1			2	2	2				8	8	8	8
3RD	10	10	2	2	2	2	2	8	8	8	8	17	17	17	
4TH	2	2	10	10	10	8	8	17	17	17	17	10	10	10	
5TH	21	7	8	8	8	17	17	10	10	10	10				
6TH	7	8	17	17	17	10	10								
7TH	8	17	2	21											
8TH	17	21	9	9											
9TH		9	12	12											
10TH		12	14	20											
11TH		14	20	14											
12TH		20													
13TH															
14TH															
15TH															
16TH															
17TH	5														
18TH															
19TH															
20TH															

RESULT

1st **4** MIKE HAWTHORN
THIN WALL SPECIAL

2nd **2** KEN WHARTON
B.R.M.

3rd **8** BOB GERARD.
COOPER BRISTOL.

Winner's Speed **92.70** m.p.h.

Fastest lap: No. **(4)**

Speed **94.53** m.p.h.

NOTE.—Where betting takes place, book-makers will pay first past the post in all races irrespective of objections.

STARTING GRID.—Fill in starting positions as announced over the loud-speakers.

2²	10³	4⁵	1¹
17	11	17
12	21	20	8
☒	14	9
16	5	21

| 4ᵗʰ 17 | 5ᵗʰ 10 | 25 6ᵗʰ 21 |

NOTICES—IMPORTANT

MOTOR RACING IS DANGEROUS

You are present at this Meeting entirely at your own risk and it is a condition of admission that all persons having any connexion with the promoters and/or organization and/or conduct of the Meeting, including the owners of the land and the drivers and owners of the vehicles and passengers in the vehicles, are absolved from all liability in respect of personal injury (whether fatal or otherwise) to you or damage to your property howsoever caused.

DOGS

In the interests of safety, dogs are not admitted to the course.

PORTABLE STANDS PROHIBITED

The organizers emphasize that spectators with improvised or portable "stands" will be refused admission.

The Goodwood Circuit, with terraced enclosures throughout almost its entire length, offers adequate views, and spectators who bring improvised "stands" interfere with the comfort of fellow spectators.

Spectators are prohibited from climbing on the roofs of any buildings in the enclosures.

Spectators occupying grandstand seats must remain seated during racing.

B.A.R.C. MEMBERS

B.A.R.C. members are reminded that there are stands available to them opposite the start, and at the Paddock Chicane. Individual seats cannot be reserved in these stands; any member is entitled to occupy a vacant seat.

Members are particularly requested to remain seated during racing.

Members and their guests are also admitted to the Paddock and to all public enclosures.

B.A.R.C. members' badges do not admit to the stands in the public enclosures.

REFRESHMENTS

Meals will be served in the Paddock marquee as follows: Breakfast, 7.45 a.m. until 10.15 a.m., price 4s.; luncheons, from 12 noon until 2.30 p.m., price 6s. Licensed bars are open from 10 a.m. and there is also a mobile bar and tea tent in the Paddock.

Breakfasts and luncheons at the same hours can be obtained in the licensed restaurant on the right of the main entrance, and set teas are served there from 3.30 p.m., price 2s.

There are marquees in all the enclosures where snacks and soft drinks, tea, coffee, etc., are served throughout the day.

Caravans: Exit times for caravans—to-day, 19th April, 6-8 p.m.; Tuesday, 20th April, up to 9 a.m. All caravans and towing vehicles must be clear of the Caravan Park by 9 a.m. on 20th April.

PROGRAMME COPYRIGHT

All literary matter in this Programme, including the list of competitors and their racing numbers, is Copyright, and any person found making illegal use thereof will be prosecuted.

The Club reserves the right to postpone, abandon, or cancel the meeting or any part thereof.

7

Some interesting Dos and Don'ts printed in the programmes. This one from 19th April 1954.

Event 2   FIVE-LAP SCRATCH RACE   2.15 p.m.

(FOR NON-SUPERCHARGED RACING CARS UP TO 2500 C.C.)

No. Entrant and Driver	Car	Cyls.	c.c.	Colour
5—R. Parnell	Ferrari	4	2490	Red
6—Ecurie Ecosse	Cooper-Bristol	6	1971	Blue
(Driver: J. Lawrence)	Cooper-Bristol	6	1971	Blue
7—Border Reivers	Cooper-Bristol	6	1971	Green
(Driver: J. Somervail)	Bristol-Alta	6	2493	Green
9—A. Wake	Maserati			
10—Gilby Engineering Co. Ltd.	Connaught	4	1967	Green
(Driver: R. F. Salvadori)	Connaught	4	1967	Green
11—M. F. Young	Connaught	4	2463	Green
12—L. Brooke	H.W.M.	4	1960	Green
14—E. N. Whiteaway	Turner			
15—J. H. Webb		4	1970	Green
(Driver: Entrant or J. E. G. Fairman)	Cooper-Alta			
16—Ecurie Richmond	Cooper-Bristol	6	1971	Green
(Driver: Eric Brandon)				
17—Ecurie Richmond		6	1996	Green
(Driver: R. Y. Nuckey)	D.H.S.			
18—C. G. H. Dunham		2	1098	Green
(Driver: G. Dunham)	Cooper-J.A.P.	4	1960	Green
21—L. Leston	Emeryson			
82—Emeryson Cars				
(Driver: P. R. Emery)				

STARTING GRID. — Fill in starting positions as announced over the loud-speakers.

10	15³	18²	
82	7⁶	5⁵	
21	11	6⁹	14
	14	15	
	17	15	
	20		

RESULT

General Classification

1st... 5
2nd... 10
3rd... 7
4th... 6
5... 11   6/82

Winner's speed:
...87.63...m.p.h.

Fastest lap:
Car No...10
at...90.95...m.p.h.

2000 c.c. Class
1st...7
2nd...6
3...11

NOTE. — Where betting takes place, bookmakers in all races will pay first past the post irrespective of objections.

19

	LAPS				
	1	2	3	4	5
1ST	5	5	5	5	5
2ND	7	10	10	10	10
3RD	10	7	7	7	7
4TH	21	21	21	11	11
5TH	11	11	11	6	6
6TH	6	6	6	82	82
7TH	18	82	82	18	18
8TH	82	18	18	15	15
9TH	15	15	15	14	14
10TH	14	14	14		
11TH					
12TH					
13TH					
14TH					
15TH					
16TH					
17TH					
18TH					
19TH					
20TH					

This typical race from the 7th June 1954 National Car Race Meeting shows the variety of cars competing on a regular basis.

Event 1   THE MADGWICK CUP   **2.00 p.m.**

(7-LAP SCRATCH RACE FOR NON-SUPERCHARGED RACING CARS
UP TO 2000 C.C.)

No. Entrant and Driver	Car	Cyls.	c.c.	Colour
11—F. R. Gerard	Cooper-Bristol	6	1971	Green/Cream
NS 12—Ecurie Richmond (Driver: R. Y. Nuckey)	Cooper-Bristol	6	1971	Green
14—Goulds Garage (Driver: H. Gould)	Cooper-Bristol	6	1971	Green
15—Equipe Devone (Driver: B. Halford)	Cooper-Bristol	6	1971	Green
16—R. Gibson	Cooper-Bristol	6	1971	Green
17—Ecurie Ecosse (Driver: P. Hughes)	Cooper-Bristol	6	1971	Blue
18—Ecurie Ecosse (Driver: J. Lawrence)	Connaught	4	1960	Blue
19—Roebuck Engineering Co. (Driver: M. F. Young)	Connaught	4	1960	Green
20—L. Marr	Connaught	4	1960	Green
21—J. Riseley-Prichard	Connaught	4	1960	Blue
22—C. D. Boulton	Connaught	4	1967	Green
23—Sir Jeremy Boles (Driver: Entrant or D. B. Beauman)	Connaught	4	1960	Green
24—R. J. Chase (Driver: Alan Brown or M. Keen)	Cooper-Alta	4	1980	Green
25—H. A. Richards	H.A.R.	6	1954	Green/Blue
26—Border Reivers (Driver: J. K. Hall)	Cooper-Bristol	6	1971	Blue
NS 46—J. H. Webb (Driver: Entrant or J. E. G. Fairman)	Turner	4	1960	Green

RESULT

STARTING GRID.—Fill in starting positions as announced over the loudspeakers.

LAP	1	2					
1st.	11	11	11	11	11	11	11
	24	24	24	23	23	23	23
2nd	21	23	23	24	24	24	24
3rd		21		21	21	21	21
4th		14		14	14	14	14

Winner's speed........86·89........m.p.h.

Fastest Lap: Car No. 23 11 at........88·34........m.p.h.

Use pages 23, 55 and 56 for lap scoring.

NOTE.—Where betting takes place, bookmakers in all races will pay first past the post irrespective of objections.

1st GERARD. — COOPER-BRISTOL.
2nd BOLES. —— CONNAUGHT.
3rd KEEN —— COOPER ALTA.
4th PRICHARD —— CONNAUGHT.

It still happens today. The man who wins pole position in practice has a very good chance of winning the race. NS = non-starter. This Madgwick Cup was held on 25th September 1954.

Event 2 **500 C.C. RACE (A)** **2.30 p.m.**

(5-LAP SCRATCH RACE FOR 500 C.C. CARS)

No.	Entrant and Driver	Car	Cyls.	c.c.	Colour
31—Cooper Car Co. Ltd. (*Driver:* S. Lewis-Evans)	... Cooper ...		1	498	Green
32—D. Parker	... Kieft ...		1	494	Maroon
34—Alan Brown ...	... Cooper ...		1	499	Silver
(*Driver:* M. Keen)	... Cooper ...		1	499	Green
35—Ecurie Richmond (*Driver:* Eric Brandon)	... Cooper ...		1	499	Green
36—Ecurie Richmond (*Driver:* R. Y. Nuckey)	... Cooper ...		1	499	Green
37—F. Beart (*Driver:* Stirling Moss)	... Cooper ...		1	497	Blue
38—D. Truman ...	... Cooper ...		1	499	Green
39—C. C. H. Davis	... Cooper ...		1	498	Red
40—J. Russell	... Cooper ...		1	499	Silver
41—R. K. Tyrrell ...	... Cooper ...		1	499	Grey
42—Ecurie Demi-litre ... (*Driver:* I. Bueb)	... Revis ...		1	500	Blue/Yellow
43—Revis Motors (*Driver:* R. G. Bicknell)	... Staride ...		1	499	Green
44—D. Taylor ...	... Staride ...		1	499	Silver
45—E. Fenning ...	... Cooper ...		1	497	Blue
47—Border Reivers (*Driver:* J. K. Hall)	... Cooper ...		1	499	Green
103-Cooper Car Co. Ltd. (*Driver:* L. Leston)					

RESULT

1st.......... 35 32 32 32 32

2nd.......... 32 35 42 37 37
40 42   43

3rd.......... 37 40 37
43   42

4th.......... 37 103
35

Winner's speed.................. 81·39 ....m.p.h.

Fastest Lap: Car No......37......at......83·88......m.p.h.

NEW RECORD LAP 500 C

Use pages 23, 55 and 56 for lap scoring.

STARTING GRID.—Fill in starting positions as announced over the loudspeakers.

35 32 40 37
103 43 42
45 41 44 34
47 38 31
36 39

NOTE.—Where betting takes place, bookmakers in all races will pay first past the post irrespective of objections.

1st D. PARKER — KIEFT
2nd S. MOSS — COOPER
3rd R. BICKNELL — REVIS.
4th I. BUEB — COOPER.

500 cc races were very popular with the spectators as cars were evenly matched and the drivers were regular competitors in this class. It was a case of close combat all the way to the line.

COMPETITION NUMBERS, ENTRANTS, CARS, ENGINE DATA AND DRIVERS

No.	Entrant	Car	Colour	No. of Cyls.	Bore and Stroke in m.m.	c.c.	Driver (1)	Driver (2)	No.
		Cars with Engines over 2000 c.c.							
1—David Brown	Aston Martin DB3S	Green	6	83 × 90	2922	R. Parnell	R. Salvadori	1
2—David Brown	Aston Martin DB3S	Green	6	83 × 90	2922	P. Collins	C. A. S. Brooks	2
3—David Brown	Aston Martin DB3S	Green	6	83 × 90	2922	P. D. C. Walker	R. D. Poore	3
4—Kangaroo Stable	Aston Martin DB3S	Green	6	83 × 90	2922	F. A. O. Gaze	D. MacKay	4
5—S. Boshier	Aston Martin DB3	Green	6	83 × 90	2922	E. W. Cuff Miller	T. Hinde	5
							Reserve: S. Boshier		
6—Marquis de Portago	Ferrari	Red	4	103 × 90	2999	Marquis de Portago	M. Hawthorn	6
7—J. Jonneret	Ferrari	Red	4	103 × 90	2999	J. Jonneret	K. Wharton	7
8—H. Schell	Ferrari	Red	4	103 × 90	2999	H. Schell	J. Lucas	8
9—J. Duncan Hamilton	Jaguar D	Green	6	83 × 106	3442	J. Duncan Hamilton	A. P. R. Rolt	9
							Reserve: P. N. Whitehead		
10—J. Duncan Hamilton	Jaguar D	Green	6	83 × 106	3442	P. N. Whitehead	M. W. Head	10
							Reserve: J. Duncan Hamilton		
11—Ecurie Ecosse	Jaguar D	Green	6	83 × 106	3442	D. Titterington	N. Sanderson	11
12—J. C. Broadhead	Jaguar D	Blue	6	83 × 106	3442	R. E. Berry	N. Dewis	12
14—John Heath	H.W.M.	Green	6	83 × 106	3442	L. Macklin	W. T. Smith	14
15—John Heath	H.W.M.	Green	6	83 × 106	3442	J. Marshall	E. Protheroe	15
16—B. E. Bradnack	Cooper-Jaguar	Green	6	83 × 106	3442	B. E. Bradnack	A. E. Marsh	16
		Cars with Engines over 1500 c.c. and up to 2000 c.c.							
21—Brian Lister (Lt. Eng.) Ltd.	Lister-Bristol	Green/White	6	66 × 96	1971	A. Moore	E. W. Holt	21
22—J. V. Green	Lister-Bristol	Green	6	66 × 96	1971	D. A. Hampshire	P. Scott-Russell	22
							Reserve: J. V. Green		
23—R. J. Chase	Cooper-Bristol	Green	6	66 × 96	1971	M. J. C. Keen	M. Anthony	23
24—T. A. D. Crook	Cooper-Bristol	Red	6	66 × 96	1971	T. A. D. Crook	R. Gibson	24
25—F. C. Davis	Lotus-Bristol	Silver	6	66 × 96	1971	F. C. Davis	R. G. Bicknell	25
26—M. Hawthorn	Tojeiro-Bristol	Green	6	66 × 96	1971	G. Rolls	J. Rolls	26
27—P. R. Crabb	Tojeiro-Bristol	Green	6	66 × 96	1971	A. P. O. Rogers	P. R. Crabb	27
28—J. R. Stoop	Frazer-Nash	Green	6	66 × 96	1971	J. R. Stoop	P. Wilson	28
		Cars with Engines up to 1500 c.c.							
30—K. McAlpine	Connaught	Green	4	75 × 84	1484	K. McAlpine	E. Thompson	30
31—Peter Bell Racing Stable	Connaught	Green	4	75 × 84	1484	L. Leston	W. A. Scott-Brown	31
32—Equipe Endeavour	Cooper-Climax	Blue	4	72 × 66	1097	T. Sopwith	P. Blond	32
33—D. J. Calvert	H.R.G.	Silver	4	73 × 90	1497	D. J. Calvert	R. C. Green	33
34—A.F.N. Ltd.	Porsche	Grey	4	86 × 66	1498	Stirling Moss	Baron von Hanstein	34
35—W. Seidel	Porsche	Silver	4	86 × 66	1498	W. Seidel	R. D. Steed	35
36—Cooper Car Co.	Cooper-Climax	Green	4	72 × 66	1097	J. Russell	I. Bueb	36
37—Panda Racing Team	Cooper-Climax	Green	4	72 × 66	1097	R. Watling-Greenwood	D. R. Barthel	37
							Reserve: M. G. H. MacDowel		
38—J. Coombs	Lotus	Green	4	75 × 84	1484	J. Coombs	J. Young	38
39—Team Lotus	Lotus	Green	4	72 × 90	1467	C. Chapman	P. Jopp	39
40—Team Lotus	Lotus	Green	4	72 × 66	1097	R. Flockhart	C. Allison	40
41—Emeryson Cars	Lotus	Silver	8	59 × 66	1493	R. A. Page	P. Emery	41
RESERVE:									
42—B. Baxter	Kieft	Green	4	73 × 89	1498	B. Baxter	H. A. Richards	42

TEAM ENTRIES: (1) Aston Martin, Cars Nos. 1, 2, 3.
(2) Ferrari, Cars Nos. 6, 7, 8.
(3) Jaguar, Cars Nos. 9, 10, 12.
(4) Cooper-Climax, Cars Nos. 32, 36, 37.
(5) Lotus, Cars Nos. 38, 39, 40.

The number of starters in the Race is limited to thirty-five.

The list of entrants, cars, and drivers for the third and, sadly, final Nine-hour race at Goodwood, held on Saturday 20th August 1955.

MEMBERSHIP FEES PAYABLE ON ENROLMENT

Applicants for membership may enrol under (*a*), (*b*) or (*c*). The fees apply irrespective of the type or h.p. of car owned. Subscriptions are renewable annually twelve months from the date of enrolment.

(*a*) B.A.R.C. membership

	£	s.	d.
Entrance Fee		10	6
Annual Subscription	1	11	6

Due on Enrolment ... £2 2 2

(*b*) Combined B.A.R.C./R.A.C. membership

	£	s.	d.
Entrance Fee		10	6
Annual Subscription	3	3	0
R.A.C. Joining Fee (covering loan of R.A.C. car badge and telephone box key)		10	6

Due on Enrolment ... £4 4 0

(*b*) includes full Associate Membership of the R.A.C. This service, which is the same as that obtained by direct Associate Membership of the R.A.C., includes the Road Guide Service, the "Get-you-home" scheme, free legal defence and advice, home and foreign touring information and assistance, and other useful services.

(*c*) B.A.R.C. Overseas membership*

	£	s.	d.
Entrance Fee		10	6
Annual Subscription	1	1	0

Due on Enrolment ... £1 11 6

* For applicants resident overseas.

B.A.R.C. MAIN FIXTURES, 1956

Apr. 7—General Practice Day, Goodwood.
Apr. 14—Members' Sports Car Meeting, Goodwood.
Apr. 21—INTERNATIONAL MEETING, AINTREE.
May 12—General Practice Day, Goodwood.
May 21—WHIT-MONDAY MEETING, GOODWOOD.
June 2—Members' Sports Car Meeting, Aintree.
June 16—EASTBOURNE RALLY.
June 23—SUMMER MEETING, AINTREE.
June 30—General Practice Day, Goodwood.
July 7—Members' Sports Car Meeting, Goodwood.
Aug. 6—BANK HOLIDAY MEETING, CRYSTAL PALACE.
Aug. 18—General Practice Day, Goodwood.
Sept. 8—SEPTEMBER MEETING, GOODWOOD.
Sept. 15—General Practice Day, Goodwood.
Sept. 22—Members' Sports Car Meeting, Goodwood.
Sept. 29—Members' Sports Car Meeting, Aintree.

The following insignia can be purchased by B.A.R.C. members: B.A.R.C. Car Badges (£1/5/0 each); Hand Embroidered Blazer Badges (Standard size 3 in. wide £2/2/0; small size 2 in. wide £1/11/6); Silk Ties (15/- each); Miniature (unmounted) Enamel Badges (Size: ¾ in. wide, 7/6 each); Enamel Lapel Badges, stud fitting (7/6 each); Enamel Brooches, pin fitting (7/6 each); Badge Transfers (6d. each). Blazer Buttons (large 2/- each,; small 1/9 each).

It can be seen from this page taken from the BARC programme of Easter Monday 2nd April 1956 that life was very different, financially, in those days.

Event 1   SPORTS CAR RACE (A)   1.33 p.m.

(26-LAP SCRATCH RACE FOR NON-SUPERCHARGED CARS NOT EXCEEDING 1500 c.c.)

No.	Entrant and Driver	Car	Cyls.	c.c.	Colour	Pit No.
24	Ecurie Demi-Litre	Lotus Climax	4	1470	Grey	(6)
	(Driver: J. M. Hawthorn)					
26	Cooper Car Co. Ltd...	Cooper Climax	4	1470	Green	(7)
	(Driver: R. F. Salvadori or J. Brabham)					
27	Cooper Car Co. Ltd...	Cooper Climax	4	1098	Green	(8)
	(Driver: M. G. H. MacDowel)					
28	Team Lotus	Lotus Climax	4	1470	Green	(9)
	(Driver: C. Chapman)					
29	Team Lotus	Lotus Climax	4	1470	Green	(10)
	(Driver: R. G. Bicknell)					
30	Team Lotus (Driver: C. Allison)	Lotus Climax	4	1098	Green	(11)
31	Border Reivers...	Lotus Climax	4	1098	Blue	(12)
	(Driver: J. Somervail)					
32	A. J. C. Mackay	Cooper Climax	4	1098	Green/Gold	(14)
33	A. E. Marsh	Cooper Climax	4	1098	Green	(15)
34	J. B. Naylor Ltd.	Maserati	4	1484	Red	(16)
	(Driver: B. Naylor)					
35	J. Coombs	Lotus Connaught	4	1496	Green	(17)
	(Driver: R. K. Tyrrell)					
36	E. Brandon	Halselec	4	1098	Green	(18)
37	E. Brandon (Driver: P. Jopp)	Halselec	4	1098	Green	(19)
38	F. W. Marriott	Lotus Climax	4	1098	Cream	(20)
39	P. H. Ashdown	Lotus Climax	4	1098	Green	(21)
40	A. Stacey	Lotus Climax	4	1098	Silver	(22)
41	Frost's (Cars) Ltd.	Lotus Climax	4	1098	Maroon	(23)
	(Driver: W. S. Frost)					
42	I. A. Forbes	Beart Rodger Climax	4	1098	White/Blue	(24)
43	D. C. T. Bennett	Fairthorpe-Climax	4	1098	Silver	(25)
44	J. Fisher	Kieft-Climax	4	1467	Blue	(26)
45	Weldangrind Ltd.	Par-son				(27)
	(Driver: S. G. Young)					
46	R. White	Lotus-M.G.	4	1467	Silver	(28)
48	R. N. Robinson (1st Reserve)	Lotus-Climax	4	1098	Silver/Green	(29)
	(Driver: Entrant or D. R. Scrutton)					
49	T. E. Watson	Lester-M.G.	6	1087	Green	(30)
	(Driver: R. B. Watson)					

RESULT

General Classification:

1st... *28 COLIN CHAPMAN*

2nd... *24 MIKE HAWTHORN*

3rd... *26 JACK BRABHAM*

4th *30 CLIFF ALLISON*

5th *27*   6th *33.*   *85·88* m.p.h.

Winner's speed... *28*&*24*   *88·71* m.p.h.

Fastest Lap: Car No...   at... m.p.h.

1100 c.c. Class:

1st...   2nd...

NOTE.—Where betting takes place, bookmakers in all races will pay first past the post irrespective of objections.

STARTING GRID.—Fill in starting positions as announced over the loud-speakers.

20 Cars   *17*

17

This entry from Whit–Monday 21st May 1956 shows that Cooper and Lotus were fighting it out but the Climax engine would win anyway. Numbers crossed through were non-starters.

Event 3 SPORTS CAR RACE (B) 3.15 p.m.

(26-LAP SCRATCH RACE FOR NON-SUPERCHARGED CARS EXCEEDING 1500 c.c.)

No. Entrant and Driver	Car	Cyls.	c.c.	Colour	Pit No.
50—Ecurie Ecosse	Jaguar D	6	3442	Blue	(6)
(Driver: D. Titterington)		6	3442	Blue	(7)
51—Ecurie Ecosse	Jaguar D	6	3442	Blue	(8)
(Driver: R. Flockhart)					
52—Ecurie Ecosse	Jaguar D	6	3442	Green	(9)
(Driver: To be nominated)					
53—J. C. Broadhead	Jaguar D	6	3442	Red	(10)
(Driver: R. E. Berry)		6	3442	Green	(11)
54—P. Blond	Jaguar D	6	3442	Green	(12)
55—I. B. Baillie	Jaguar D				
56—G. Abecassis JACK FAIRMAN	H.W.M.	6	1985	Green/Yellow.	(14)
(Driver: J. M. Hawthorn)					
57—Brian Lister (Light Eng.) Ltd.	Lister Maserati	6	3442	White	(15)
(Driver: W. A. Scott-Brown)	Cooper-Jaguar	6	3442	Green	(16)
58—M. W. Head	Cooper-Jaguar	6	3442	Blue	(17)
59—R. D. Steed	Jaguar XK120C				
60—Kieft Sports Car Co.					(18)
(Driver: J. M. Trimble)	Aston Martin DB3S	6	2922	Green	(19)
61—The Vermin Stable					
(Driver: J. E. G. Stevens)	Aston Martin DB3S	6	2922	Green	(20)
62—Equipe Devone		6	3442	Green	
(Driver: T. Kyffin)	Jaguar XK120C				(21)
63—M. Charles Motors Ltd.		6	1971	Silver	(22)
(Driver: M. Charles)	Lotus-Bristol	6	1971	Silver	
64—F. C. Davis	Lotus Bristol				(23)
65—The Augean Stable		6	1971	Silver	(24)
(Driver: M. Anthony or C. M. Lund)	Tojeiro Bristol	6	1971	Green	(25)
66—P. R. Crabb	Frazer-Nash	6	1971	Green	
67—R. J. W. Utley	Lister Bristol				(26)
68—O. Issard-Davies		6	1991	Green	
(Driver: A. Moore)	A.C.				(27)
69—R. N. Robinson		4	2660	Blue	
(Driver: Entrant or E. G. Vaughan)	Austin Healey				
70—J. E. Burgess					

RESULT

1st. 53 BOB BERRY

2nd. 51 RON FLOCKHART

3rd. 50 DES TITTERINGTON

4th. 56 JACK FAIRMAN

55 59 6/58

Winner's speed. 42-37sec. 87·85 m.p.h.

Fastest Lap: Car No. 51 at 89·26 m.p.h.

2000 CLASS:

1st. 64 2nd. 68

NOTE.—Where betting takes place, bookmakers in all races will pay first past the post irrespective of objections.

21

STARTING GRID.—Fill in starting positions as announced over the loud-speakers.

59¹	56²	57³	53⁴
66⁵	60⁶	65⁷	
54⁸	51⁹	50¹⁰	69¹¹
58¹²	57¹³	55¹⁴	
67¹⁵	64¹⁶	62¹⁷	61¹⁸
21		68	

This race, also from 21st May 1956, was very much a Jaguar benefit. I believe that the HWM had a Jaguar engine also. Numbers crossed through were non-starters.

Event 6   THE GOODWOOD TROPHY   **4.45 p.m.**
(21-LAP SCRATCH RACE FOR NON-SUPERCHARGED SPORTS CARS
EXCEEDING 1500 c.c.)

No. Entrant and Driver	Car	Cyls.	c.c.	Colour
1—Ecurie Ecosse (Driver: R. Flockhart)	Jaguar D	6	3442	Blue
2—Ecurie Ecosse (Driver: N. Sanderson)	Jaguar D	6	3442	Blue
3—Ecurie Ecosse (Driver: J. Lawrence)	Jaguar D	6	3442	Blue
4—J. C. Broadhead (Driver: R. E. Berry)	Jaguar D	6	3442	Green
5—David Brown (Driver: R. Salvadori)	Aston Martin DB3S	6	2922	Green
6—David Brown (Driver: C. A. S. Brooks)	Aston Martin DB3S	6	2922	Green
7—A. N. Other	To be nominated	6	2922	Green
8—A. G. Whitehead	Aston Martin DB3S	6	2922	Green
9—Equipe Devone (Driver: T. T. Kyffin)	Aston Martin DB3S	6	2922	Orange
10—Hans Davids	H.W.M.	6	3442	Green
11—H. W. Motors Ltd. (Driver: N. Cunningham Reid)	H.W.M.	6	3442	Green
12—H. W. Motors Ltd. (Driver: E. Protheroe)	Lister-Maserati	6	1985	Green/Yellow
14—Brian Lister (Light Eng.) Ltd. (Driver: W. A. Scott Brown)	Jaguar D	6	3442	Red
15—P. Blond	Jaguar-XK120C	6	3442	Blue
16—J. M. Trimble	Aston Martin-Jaguar	6	3442	Green
17—R. H. Dennis (Driver: G. N. Richardson)	Tojeiro-Jaguar	6	3442	Green
18—Tojeiro Car Co. (Driver: To be nominated)	Cooper-Jaguar	6	3442	Green
19—R. D. Steed	Cooper-Jaguar	6	3442	White
20—M. W. Head	Lotus-Bristol	6	1971	Green
21—F. C. Davis	Lotus-Bristol	6	1971	Green/White
22—M. Anthony (Driver: C. M. Lund)	Tojeiro-Bristol	6	1971	Silver
23—P. R. Crabb				

(The pits are numbered to correspond with race numbers.)

RESULT

6. 1st Tony Brooks DB3S.
5. 2nd Roy Salvadori DB3S.
1. 3rd Ron Flockhart Jaguar D
11. 4th Noel C. Reid H.W.M.
2. 5th Ninian Sanderson Jaguar D
3. 6th J. Lawrence Jaguar.

Winner's speed....................m.p.h.

Fastest Lap: Car No. 2 at 89.07 m.p.h.

Use opposite page for lap scoring.

NOTE.—Where betting takes place, bookmakers in all races will pay first past the post irrespective of objections.

37

STARTING GRID.—Fill in starting positions as announced over the loud-speakers.

2-litre Class.
21. F. C. Davis (Lotus-Bristol) 20 Laps.

Compared to the previous page, this one from the 8th September meeting of 1956 shows that Aston Martin were not going to let Jaguar have things all their own way.

Although raced by their makers today, these Formula 2 Cooper and Lotus cars will be on sale to private entrants and, for comparatively reasonable sums, according to established motor racing costs, will enable many drivers to graduate to racing cars, as opposed to sports cars. The availability of these new models depends largely on the Coventry-Climax factory's ability to turn out the engines.

Another British design, not yet completed, is the Lister-Climax, using the same engine and having a layout similar to that of the Lotus.

Abroad, Gordini of France is said to be already working on a Formula 2 car, using an existing 1½-litre sports car engine, while Porsche and Borgward of Germany and Maserati of Italy all have suitable capacity sports car engines but are not, apparently, as yet interested in the Formula.

Ferrari of Italy are reported to have virtually completed their Formula 2 model and in doing so have already pointed out the danger both to the intentions of Formula 2 and to the continuation of Formula 1.

The Ferrari is said to be a most complex machine, with a "V-6" engine, each bank of three cylinders having twin-overhead camshafts, and developing already over 180 b.h.p. at some phenomenal crankshaft speed, with even more power as a possibility.

Such a machine is likely to be extremely expensive, compared with the quite simple British designs, and beyond the financial resources of the type of driver at present contemplating Formula 2 racing. There is also the possibility that, in going all out to build a world-beating Formula 2 car, a designer will make it even faster than his own Formula 1 model, causing the death of the present Formula 1 and the substitution of Formula 2 races for the World Championship events, as happened in 1953.

B.A.R.C. MEMBERS

B.A.R.C. members and their guests holding Goodwood season brooch sets or day tickets are reminded that there are seats available for them in the stands opposite the start line and pits as well as at the Paddock Chicane. Individual seats cannot be reserved in these stands. Any member or guest is entitled to occupy a vacant seat. It is the organizers' intention that members and guests should be able to see the racing from different vantage points during the meeting and not be tied to any particular seat.

*   *   *

Members and guests, when leaving their seats for any substantial length of time, are requested not to attempt to "reserve" them by leaving hats and coats behind.

*   *   *

Members and their guests are admitted to the Paddock and to all public enclosures. B.A.R.C. members' or guests' badges do **not** admit to the stands in the public enclosures.

*   *   *

Stand occupants are earnestly requested to remain seated during racing.

Refreshments.—A members' restaurant is located in the former Flying Control building opposite the start, where luncheons will be served from 12 noon until 2.30 p.m. (price 8s. 6d.) and teas (3s.) from 3 p.m. onwards. There is a licensed bar adjoining. Refreshments are also available in the Paddock.

*   *   *

The rest of the Goodwood season for B.A.R.C. members is:

Sat., Apr. 27—*Practice Day.*
Sat., May 11—25th Members' Meeting.
Sat., May 18—*Practice Day.*
Whit-Monday, June 10—NATIONAL MEETING
Sat., June 22—26th Members' Meeting.
Sat., July 27—*Practice Day.*
Sat., Aug. 10—*Practice Day.*
Sat., Aug. 31—27th Members' Meeting.
Sat., Sept. 28—NATIONAL MEETING.

*   *   *

Members (other than Goodwood season brooch holders) and their guests will require tickets for the Members' Meetings. Apply in advance to the General Secretary, B.A.R.C., 55 Park Lane, W.1.

*   *   *

Ticket applications for the Whit-Monday and 28th September National Meetings should be made on the forms circulated by the Club before each meeting.

18

When time allowed (usually long after the meeting) the introductory pages of the BARC Goodwood programmes made interesting reading—this one from Easter Monday 22nd April 1957.

Goodwood Circuit and Class Records

LAP RECORD FOR THE PRESENT CIRCUIT:

Stirling Moss (Maserati), 1 min. 30.2 sec., 95.79 m.p.h. (Richmond Formula 1 Race, April 1956).

RACING CAR CLASS RECORDS:

A Over 8000 c.c.:
B Exceeding 5000 c.c. and up to 8000 c.c.: S. H. Allard (Allard), 1 min. 47.2 sec., 80.60 m.p.h.
C Exceeding 3000 c.c. and up to 5000 c.c.; J. M. Hawthorn (Ferrari Thin Wall Special), 1 min. 31.4 sec., 94.53 m.p.h.
D Exceeding 2000 c.c. and up to 3000 c.c.: Stirling Moss (Maserati), 1 min. 30.2 sec., 95.79 m.p.h.
E Exceeding 1500 c.c. and up to 2000 c.c.: R. F. Salvadori (Connaught), 1 min. 34.2 sec., 91.72 m.p.h.
F Exceeding 1100 c.c. and up to 1500 c.c.: J. M. Fangio (B.R.M. s/c.), 1 min. 32.2 sec., 93.71 m.p.h.
G Exceeding 750 c.c. and up to 1100 c.c.: L. Leston (Cooper), 1 min. 42.3 sec., 84.37 m.p.h.
H Exceeding 500 c.c. and up to 750 c.c.:
I Exceeding 350 c.c. and up to 500 c.c.: J. Russell (Cooper), 1 min. 41.8 sec., 84.87 m.p.h.

BEST SPORTS CAR TIME:

J. M. Hawthorn (Ferrari, Nine Hours Race, 1955); 1 min. 34.8 sec., 91.14 m.p.h.

SPORTS CAR CLASS RECORDS:

A Over 8000 c.c.:
B Exceeding 5000 c.c. and up to 8000 c.c.:
C Exceeding 3000 c.c. and up to 5000 c.c.: J. D. Titterington (Jaguar D), 1 min. 36.6 sec., 89.44 m.p.h.
D Exceeding 2000 c.c. and up to 3000 c.c.: J. M. Hawthorn (Ferrari), 1 min. 34.8 sec., 91.14 m.p.h.
E Exceeding 1500 c.c. and up to 2000 c.c.: W. A. Scott-Brown (Lister-Maserati) 1 min. 38.6 sec., 87.64 m.p.h.
F Exceeding 1100 c.c. and up to 1500 c.c.: J. M. Hawthorn (Lotus-Climax), 1 min. 36.8 sec., 89.26 m.p.h.
G Exceeding 750 c.c. and up to 1100 c.c.: J. K. Hall (Lotus-Climax), 1 min. 39.2 sec., 87.10 m.p.h.
H Exceeding 500 c.c. and up to 750 c.c.: D. R. Piper (Lotus M.G. s/c.), 1 min. 57.2 sec., 73.72 m.p.h.

Some Fast Goodwood Laps

(RACING CARS)

							m. sec.	m.p.h.
1948—September	F. R. Gerard (E.R.A.)	...	...	...	...	...	1 43.6	83.40
1949—April (*Easter*)	Reg. Parnell (Maserati s/c.)	...	...	...	...		1 39.2	87.10
" —September ...	Reg. Parnell (Maserati s/c.)	...	...	...			1 36.8	89.26
1950—April (*Easter*)	P. D. C. Walker (E Type E.R.A. s/c.)	...					1 43.8	83.24
" —May (*Whitsun*)	Brian Shawe-Taylor (E.R.A. s/c.)						1 40.2	86.22
" —September ...	Reg. Parnell (B.R.M. s/c.)						1 41.8	84.87
1951—March (*Easter*)	"B. Bira" (O.S.C.A.)	...					1 35.6	90.38
" —May (*Whitsun*)	Reg. Parnell (Thin Wall Special)						1 31.4	94.53
" —September ...	Giuseppe Farina (Alfa-Romeo s/c.)						1 28.0	97.36
*1952—April (*Easter*)	J. Froilan Gonzalez (Ferrari Thin Wall Special)					1 36.0	90.00
" —June (*Whitsun*)	J. M. Hawthorn (Cooper-Bristol)						1 39.0	87.27
" —September ...	Reg. Parnell (B.R.M. s/c.)	...	...	...			1 35.6	90.38
1953—April (*Easter*)	Ken Wharton (B.R.M. s/c.)						1 33.8	92.11
" —September ...	J. M. Hawthorn (Ferrari Thin Wall Special) ...					1 31.4	94.53
1954—April (*Easter*)	K. Wharton (B.R.M. s/c.)						1 35.6	90.38
" —June (*Whitsun*)	Peter Collins (Ferrari Thin Wall Special)					1 32.6	93.30
" —September ...	Peter Collins (Ferrari Thin Wall Special)					1 32.3	93.71
1955—April (*Easter*)	Peter Collins (B.R.M. s/c.)						1 33.0	92.90
1956—April (*Easter*)	Stirling Moss (Maserati) ...						1 30.2	95.79

(* The Paddock chicane was first used at this meeting.)

19

For those readers interested in facts and figures, this page from Easter Monday 22nd April 1957 also makes interesting reading.

Event 4 GOODWOOD TROPHY 3.45 p.m.

(21-LAP SCRATCH RACE (LE MANS TYPE START) FOR NON-SUPERCHARGED
SPORTS CARS OF UNLIMITED ENGINE CAPACITY)

Pit numbers correspond with competition numbers

No.	Entrant and Driver	Car	Cyls.	c.c.	Colour
1	Murkett Bros. Ltd... (*Driver:* H. C. Taylor)	Jaguar D	6	3442	White
2	J. Duncan Hamilton	Jaguar D	6	3779	Green
3	Maurice Charles Motors Ltd. (*Driver:* M. Charles)	Jaguar D	6	3442	Blue
6	P. Mould	Jaguar XK120C	6	3442	Green
7	Brian Lister (Lt. Eng.) Ltd. (*Driver:* W. A. Scott-Brown)	Lister-Jaguar	6	3781	Green/Yellow
8	Equipe Devone (*Driver:* T. T. Kyffin)	Lister-Jaguar ...	6	3442	Green
9	H.W. Motors Ltd. (*Driver:* P. Blond)	H.W.M.-Jaguar	6	3442	Green
10	H.W. Motors Ltd. (*Driver:* To be nominated)	H.W.M.-Jaguar	6	3442	Green
11	Tojeiro Car Co. (*Driver:* To be nominated)	Tojeiro-Jaguar	6	3442	Green
12	Tojeiro Car Co. (*Driver:* To be nominated)	Tojeiro-Jaguar	6	3442	White
14	M. W. Head	Cooper-Jaguar	6	3442	Red
15	D. S. Shale ...	Cooper-Jaguar	6	2922	Green
16	P. N. Whitehead	Aston Martin DB3S...	6	2922	Green
17	A. G. Whitehead	Aston Martin DB3S...	6	2922	Blue
18	J. F. Dalton...	Aston Martin DB3S...	8	4640	Green/White
19	W. Sadler	Sadler Special	6	1993	Green/Red
20	J. B. Naylor Ltd. (*Driver:* B. Naylor)	Lotus-Maserati	6	1971	Silver
21	P. R. Crabb...	Tojeiro-Bristol	4	1460	Blue
22	J. Coombs (*Driver:* R. Salvadori) ...	Lotus-Climax...	4	1460	Silver/Green
23	W. S. Frost ...	Lotus-Climax...	4	1490	Red
24	P. H. Brolen	O.S.C.A.	4	1460	Green
25	Team Lotus (*Driver:* C. Allison) ...	Lotus-Climax...	4	1460	Green
26	Team Lotus (*Driver:* G. Hill)	Lotus-Climax...	4	1460	Blue
27	Equipe Endeavour (*Driver:* Sir Gawaine Baillie)	Lotus-Climax...	4	1098	Green
28	R. C. Robinson (*Driver:* I. Ireland) ...	Lotus-Climax...	4	1098	Silver/Green
29	D. Piper	Lotus-Climax...	4	1098	Green
30	J. Campbell Jones ... (Reserve) (*Driver:* Entrant or H. J. Fredman)				

RESULT

7 1st ARCHIE SCOTT-BROWN 11 2nd. JACK BRABHAM TOJEIRO-JAG WORKS
WORKS LISTER-JAGUAR

1 3rd. HENRY TAYLOR JAGUAR-D 22 4th. ROY SALVADORI J. COOMBS LOTUS CLIMAX
MURKETT BROS.

2 5th. J. DUNCAN HAMILTON JAGUAR-D

Winner's speed.....................m.p.h.   Fastest Lap: Car No.........at.........m.p.h.

2000 CLASS:

1st.....................   2nd.....................

Speed.....................m.p.h.

Use page 35 for lap scoring.

NOTE.—Where betting takes place, bookmakers in all races will pay first past the post
irrespective of objections.

37

A good variety of cars and drivers for the Goodwood Trophy Race of 28th September 1957, and once
again Archie Scott-Brown and the Lister-Jaguar could not be caught. We must have had rain judging from
the marks on the paper.

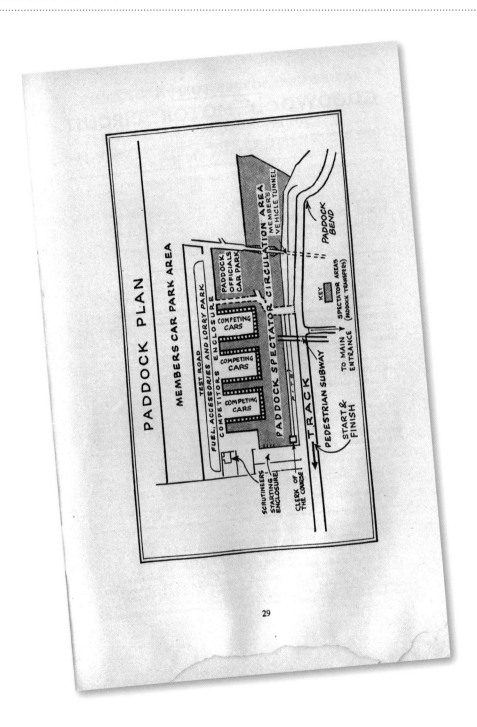

29

The paddock lay-out as it was by the end of the 1950s, this page taken from the BARC Programme for the Easter Monday meeting, 7th April 1958.

COMING EVENTS AT GOODWOOD

34th B.A.R.C. Members' Meeting, Saturday, 25th April. First race: 2 p.m.

SOMETIMES known as "the class-room of British motor racing", B.A.R.C. members' meetings at Goodwood provide many drivers with their first opportunity to race, while other drivers of greater experience regard these meetings as the most enjoyable form of motor racing in which they take part.

Either way, the racing is usually blessed with some extremely keen competition in the scratch and handicap events which are contested by large fields of a wide variety of cars—sports racing, saloons, production type sports cars and "specials".

Prices for this meeting (not bookable in advance) are:

Public Enclosures	...	...	...	4/-
Children (under 14)	...	...	...	2/6
Transfer to Stands	...	...	...	2/6 (unreserved)
(No reduction for children)				
Transfer to Paddock	...	...	...	5/-
(No reduction for children)				
Car Parks	...	...	...	5/- and 2/6
Coaches	...	...	...	10/-
Motor Cycles	...	...	...	2/6

Note: Details of the special admission arrangements available to B.A.R.C. Members have been advised in the Club's diary fixture list. Members should apply for tickets by 22nd April latest.

National Meeting, Whit-Monday, 18th May. First Race: 1.30 p.m.

AT Goodwood on Whit-Monday a mixed programme of races has been arranged in which racing, sports and saloon cars will be seen in a variety of events. A popular feature of this meeting is likely to be the race for "historic" racing cars in which the models which thrilled the crowds in the early days of Goodwood will be seen once again and can be compared with the very latest in motor racing machinery. Watch the daily and motoring Press for further details. An application form for public tickets appears opposite.

Note: Special admission arrangements are available for B.A.R.C. Members, who should apply for tickets on the form to be circulated direct to them.

R.A.C. Tourist Trophy Race, Saturday, 26th September

ONCE again the Tourist Trophy Race comes to Goodwood to stage the British round in the World Sports Car Championship and bring the finest drivers and sports cars in the world to the Sussex track to do battle in the only long-distance sports car classic race to be held in England during the season.

This is the oldest surviving motor race, having been first held in the Isle of Man in 1905, and has been won by such famous drivers as the Hon. Charles Rolls, K. Lee Guinness, Kaye Don, Rudolf Caracciola, Tazio Nuvolari, Freddie Dixon, Peter Collins and (four times) Stirling Moss.

Application forms for this great meeting will be circulated well in advance.

Public ticket prices will be as follows:

Public Enclosures	...	...	...	7/6
Children (under 14)	...	...	...	4/-
Transfer to Stands	...	...	...	22/6
(No reduction for children)				
Transfer to Paddock	...	...	...	22/6
(No reduction for children)				
Car Parks	...	...	...	10/- and 5/-
Coaches	...	...	...	10/-
Motor Cycles	...	...	...	2/6

All tickets for the T.T., except 5/- car parking and motor cycle parking, are available in advance from the B.A.R.C. Office, at 18 South Street, London, W.1.

19

Some more interesting facts, figures, and information from the programme pages of 30th April 1959.

SPEED TABLE

1 lap = 2.4 miles

Lap Time M. S.	Speed M.P.H.	Lap Time M. S.	Speed M.P.H.	Lap Time M. S.	Speed M.P.H.	Lap Time M. S.	Speed M.P.H.
1 29	97.08	1 38	88.16	1 47	80.75	1 56	74.48
.2	96.86	.2	87.98	.2	80.60	.2	74.35
.4	96.64	.4	87.80	.4	80.45	.4	74.23
.6	96.43	.6	87.63	.6	80.30	.6	74.10
18	96.21	.8	87.45	.8	80.15	.8	73.97
1 30	96.00	1 39	87.27	1 48	80.00	1 57	73.85
.2	95.79	.2	87.10	.2	79.85	.2	73.72
.4	95.57	.4	86.92	.4	79.70	.4	73.59
.6	95.36	.6	86.75	.6	79.56	.6	73.47
.8	95.15	.8	86.57	.8	79.41	.8	73.34
1 31	94.94	1 40	86.40	1 49	79.27	1 58	73.22
12	94.74	.2	86.22	.2	79.12	.2	73.10
.4	94.53	.4	86.06	.4	78.98	.4	72.97
.6	94.32	.6	85.88	.6	78.83	.6	72.85
.8	94.12	.8	85.71	.8	78.69	.8	72.73
1 32	93.91	1 41	85.54	1 50	78.54	1 59	72.60
.2	93.71	.2	85.37	.2	78.40	.2	72.48
.4	93.51	.4	85.21	.4	78.26	.4	72.36
.6	93.30	.6	85.04	.6	78.12	.6	72.24
.8	93.10	.8	84.87	.8	77.98	.8	72.12
1 33	92.90	1 42	84.71	1 51	77.84	2 0	72.00
.2	92.70	.2	84.54	.2	77.70	.2	71.88
.4	92.50	.4	84.37	.4	77.56	.4	71.76
.6	92.31	.6	84.21	.6	77.42	.6	71.64
.8	92.11	.8	84.05	.8	77.28	.8	71.52
1 34	91.91	1 43	83.88	1 52	77.14	2 01	71.40
.2	91.72	.2	83.72	.2	77.00	.2	71.29
.4	91.52	.4	83.56	.4	76.87	.4	71.17
.6	91.33	.6	83.40	.6	76.73	.6	71.05
.8	91.14	.8	83.24	.8	76.60	.8	70.94
1 35	90.95	1 44	83.08	1 53	76.46	2 02	70.82
.2	90.76	.2	82.92	.2	76.32	.2	70.70
.4	90.57	.4	82.76	.4	76.19	.4	70.59
.6	90.38	.6	82.60	.6	76.06	.6	70.47
.8	90.19	.8	82.44	.8	75.92	.8	70.36
1 36	90.00	1 45	82.29	1 54	75.79	2 03	70.24
.2	89.81	.2	82.13	.2	75.66	.2	70.13
.4	89.63	.4	81.97	.4	75.52	.4	70.02
.6	89.44	.6	81.82	.6	75.39	.6	69.90
.8	89.26	.8	81.66	.8	75.26	.8	69.79
1 37	89.07	1 46	81.51	1 55	75.13	2 04	69.68
.2	88.89	.2	81.36	.2	75.00	.2	69.56
.4	88.71	.4	81.20	.4	74.87	.4	69.45
.6	88.52	.6	81.05	.6	74.74	.6	69.34
.8	88.3	.8	80.90	.8	74.61	.8	69.23

The Goodwood Speed Table—still relevant today.

GOODWOOD SPEED TABLE

Lap Time M.S.	Speed M.P.H.	Lap Time M.S.	Speed M.P.H.	Lap Time M.S.	Speed M.P.H.	Lap Time M.S.	Speed M.P.H.
2 05	69.12	2 09	66.98	2 13	64.96	2 17	63.07
.2	69.01	.2	66.87	.2	64.86	.2	62.97
.4	68.90	.4	66.77	.4	64.77	.4	62.88
.6	68.79	.6	66.67	.6	64.67	.6	62.79
.8	68.68	.8	66.56	.8	64.57	.8	62.70
2 06	68.57	2 10	66.46	2 14	64.48	2 18	62.61
.2	68.46	.2	66.36	.2	64.38	.2	62.52
.4	68.35	.4	66.26	.4	64.29	.4	62.43
.6	68.25	.6	66.16	.6	64.19	.6	62.34
.8	68.14	.8	66.05	.8	64.09	.8	62.25
2 07	68.03	2 11	65.95	2 15	64.00	2 19	62.16
.2	67.92	.2	65.85	.2	63.90	.2	62.07
.4	67.82	.4	65.75	.4	63.81	.4	61.98
.6	67.71	.6	65.65	.6	63.72	.6	61.89
.8	67.61	.8	65.55	.8	63.62	.8	61.80
2 08	67.50	2 12	65.45	2 16	63.53	2 20	61.71
.2	67.39	.2	65.35	.2	63.44		
.4	67.29	.4	65.26	.4	63.34		
.6	67.18	.6	65.16	.6	63.25		
.8	67.08	.8	65.06	.8	63.16		

 *International Flag Signals*

Red: Signal for complete and immediate stop. **Yellow** (*Waved*): Great danger, be prepared to stop. **Yellow** (*Motionless*): Take care, danger. **Yellow with Vertical Red Stripes:** Take care, oil has been spilled somewhere on the road. **Blue** (*Waved*): Another competitor is trying to overtake you. **Blue** (*Motionless*): Another competitor is following you very closely. **White:** An ambulance or service car is on the circuit. **Black** (*with Competitor's Number*): Signal for the competitor to stop on the n⋯ circuit. **Black and White Chequered:** Signal for the winner and end of the race. T⋯ Union Jack will be used for starting signals.

Y

A number of the photographs and drawings throughout the book include vehicle registration numbers. This index lists those we have been able to identify. In some cases a "?" is used to indicate an unreadable character.